THE
IMMIGRANT
EXPERIENCE

The Peoples of North America

THE
IMMIGRANT
EXPERIENCE

David M. Reimers

CHELSEA HOUSE PUBLISHERS

New York   Philadelphia

On the cover: Immigrants look toward Liberty Island in New York Harbor.

Chelsea House Publishers
Editor-in-Chief: Nancy Toff
Executive Editor: Remmel T. Nunn
Managing Editor: Karyn Gullen Browne
Copy Chief: Juliann Barbato
Picture Editor: Adrian G. Allen
Art Director: Maria Epes
Manufacturing Manager: Gerald Levine

The Peoples of North America
Senior Editor: Sean Dolan

Staff for THE IMMIGRANT EXPERIENCE
Associate Editor: Abigail Meisel
Deputy Copy Chief: Ellen Scordato
Editorial Assistant: Elizabeth Nix
Picture Research: PAR/NYC
Assistant Art Director: Laurie Jewell
Senior Designer: Noreen M. Lamb
Production Coordinator: Joseph Romano
Cover Illustration: Paul Biniasz
Banner Design: Hrana L. Janto

First Printing

1 3 5 7 9 8 6 4 2

Library of Congress Cataloging-in-Publication Data
Reimers, David M.
  The Immigrant Experience

  (The Peoples of North America)
  Bibliography: p.
  Includes index.
  1. North America—Emigration and immigration.
2. Immigrants—North America. I. Title. II. Series.
JV6137.R45 1988   325.7   87-31482
ISBN 0-87754-881-1
     0-7910-0295-0 (pbk.)

CONTENTS

THE PEOPLES OF NORTH AMERICA

CHELSEA HOUSE PUBLISHERS

A
NATION
OF
NATIONS

Daniel Patrick Moynihan

The Constitution of the United States begins: "We the People of the United States . . ." Yet, as we know, the United States is not made up of a single group of people. It is made up of many peoples. Immigrants from Europe, Asia, Africa, and Central and South America settled in North America seeking a new life filled with opportunities unavailable in their homeland. Coming from many nations, they forged one nation and made it their own. More than 100 years ago, Walt Whitman expressed this perception of America as a melting pot: "Here is not merely a nation, but a teeming Nation of nations."

Although the ingenuity and acts of courage of these immigrants, our ancestors, shaped the North American way of life, we sometimes take their contributions for granted. This fine series, *The Peoples of North America,* examines the experiences and contributions of the immigrants and how these contributions determined the future of the United States and Canada.

Immigrants did not abandon their ethnic traditions when they reached the shores of North America. Each ethnic group had its own customs and traditions, and each brought different experiences, accomplishments, skills, values, styles of dress, and tastes in food that lingered long after its arrival. Yet this profusion of differences created a singularity, or bond, among the immigrants.

The United States and Canada are unusual in this respect. Whereas religious and ethnic differences have sparked intolerance throughout the rest of the world—from the 17th-century religious wars to the 19th-century nationalist movements in Europe to the near extermination of the Jewish people under Nazi Germany—North Americans have struggled to learn how to respect each other's differences and live in harmony.

Millions of immigrants from scores of homelands brought diversity to our continent. In a mass migration, some 12 million immigrants passed through the waiting rooms of New York's Ellis Island; thousands more came to the West Coast. At first, these immigrants were welcomed because labor was needed to meet the demands of the Industrial Age. Soon, however, the new immigrants faced the prejudice of earlier immigrants who saw them as a burden on the economy. Legislation was passed to limit immigration. The Chinese Exclusion Act of 1882 was among the first laws closing the doors to the promise of America. The Japanese were also effectively excluded by this law. In 1924, Congress set immigration quotas on a country-by-country basis.

Such prejudices might have triggered war, as they did in Europe, but North Americans chose negotiation and compromise, instead. This determination to resolve differences peacefully has been the hallmark of the peoples of North America.

The remarkable ability of Americans to live together as one people was seriously threatened by the issue of slavery. It was a symptom of growing intolerance in the world. Thousands of settlers from the British Isles had arrived in the colonies as indentured servants, agreeing to work for a specified number of years on farms or as apprentices in return for passage to America and room and board. When the first Africans arrived in the then-British colonies during the 17th century, some colonists thought that they too should be treated as indentured servants. Eventually, the question of whether the Africans should be viewed as indentured, like the English, or as slaves who could be owned for life, was considered in a Maryland court. The court's calamitous decree held that blacks were slaves bound to lifelong servitude, and so were their children.

America went through a time of moral examination and civil war before it finally freed African slaves and their descendants. The principle that all people are created equal had faced its greatest challenge and survived.

Yet the court ruling that set blacks apart from other races fanned flames of discrimination that burned long after slavery was abolished—and that still flicker today. The concept of racism had existed for centuries in countries throughout the world. For instance, when the Manchus conquered China in the 17th century, they decreed that Chinese and Manchus could not intermarry. To impress their superiority on the conquered Chinese, the Manchus ordered all Chinese men to wear their hair in a long braid called a queue.

By the 19th century, some intellectuals took up the banner of racism, citing Charles Darwin. Darwin's scientific studies hypothesized that highly evolved animals were dominant over other animals. Some advocates of this theory applied it to humans, asserting that certain races were more highly evolved than others and thus were superior.

This philosophy served as the basis for a new form of discrimination, not only against nonwhite people but also against various ethnic groups. Asians faced harsh discrimination and were depicted by popular 19th-century newspaper cartoonists as depraved, degenerate, and deficient in intelligence. When the Irish flooded American cities to escape the famine in Ireland, the cartoonists caricatured the typical "Paddy" (a common term for Irish immigrants) as an apelike creature with jutting jaw and sloping forehead.

By the 20th century, racism and ethnic prejudice had given rise to virulent theories of a Northern European master race. When Adolf Hitler came to power in Germany in 1933, he popularized the notion of Aryan supremacy. "Aryan," a term referring to the Indo-European races, was applied to so-called superior physical characteristics such as blond hair, blue eyes, and delicate facial features. Anyone with darker and heavier features was considered inferior. Buttressed by these theories, the German Nazi state from

1933 to 1945 set out to destroy European Jews, along with Poles, Russians, and other groups considered inferior. It nearly succeeded. Millions of these people were exterminated.

The tragedies brought on by ethnic and racial intolerance throughout the world demonstrate the importance of North America's efforts to create a society free of prejudice and inequality.

A relatively recent example of the New World's desire to resolve ethnic friction nonviolently is the solution the Canadians found to a conflict between two ethnic groups. A long-standing dispute as to whether Canadian culture was properly English or French resurfaced in the mid-1960s, dividing the peoples of the French-speaking Quebec Province from those of the English-speaking provinces. Relations grew tense, then bitter, then violent. The Royal Commission on Bilingualism and Biculturalism was established to study the growing crisis and to propose measures to ease the tensions. As a result of the commission's recommendations, all official documents and statements from the national government's capital at Ottawa are now issued in both French and English, and bilingual education is encouraged.

The year 1980 marked a coming of age for the United States's ethnic heritage. For the first time, the U.S. Census asked people about their ethnic background. Americans chose from more than 100 groups, including French Basque, Spanish Basque, French Canadian, Afro-American, Peruvian, Armenian, Chinese, and Japanese. The ethnic group with the largest response was English (49.6 million). More than 100 million Americans claimed ancestors from the British Isles, which includes England, Ireland, Wales, and Scotland. There were almost as many Germans (49.2 million) as English. The Irish-American population (40.2 million) was third, but the next largest ethnic group, the Afro-Americans, was a distant fourth (21 million). There was a sizable group of French ancestry (13 million), as well as of Italian (12 million). Poles, Dutch, Swedes, Norwegians, and Russians followed. These groups, and other smaller ones, represent the wondrous profusion of ethnic influences in North America.

Canada, too, has learned more about the diversity of its population. Studies conducted during the French/English conflict showed that Canadians were descended from Ukrainians, Germans, Italians, Chinese, Japanese, native Indians, and Eskimos, among others. Canada found it had no ethnic majority, although nearly half of its immigrant population had come from the British Isles. Canada, like the United States, is a land of immigrants for whom mutual tolerance is a matter of reason as well as principle.

The people of North America are the descendants of one of the greatest migrations in history. And that migration is not over. Koreans, Vietnamese, Nicaraguans, Cubans, and many others are heading for the shores of North America in large numbers. This mix of cultures shapes every aspect of our lives. To understand ourselves, we must know something about our diverse ethnic ancestry. Nothing so defines the North American nations as the motto on the Great Seal of the United States: *E Pluribus Unum*—Out of Many, One. ✎

The Puritans of New England walk to church in this 1867 historical painting by British artist George Henry Boughton.

A CONTINENT DIVIDED

When Spanish explorers sailed to the shores of North America in the 16th century, they encountered people who had already lived there for thousands of years. No one knows exactly when these earliest inhabitants of North America—Native Americans—first arrived on the continent, but most anthropologists date their migration back to 15,000–40,000 years ago. Scholars have a clearer idea of *how* Native Americans came than *when* they came: They migrated on foot from northeast Asia over a period of thousands of years, crossing a land bridge that once linked Siberia and Alaska. In time the seas swallowed up this land passage, and in its place now stands the Bering Strait, a narrow waterway running between Siberia and North America.

These early Americans left no written records as they scattered across what is now Canada and the United States and headed south into the areas that were to become Mexico and South America, but it is almost certain that they lived as nomads. They kept on the move constantly, crossing hundreds of miles to hunt wild animals and gather the edible plants that supplemented their diet. Native Americans roamed the continent for several thousand years, but in about 8,000 B.C.—approximately 10,000 years ago—they began to

Indians of the village of Secoton, located near Roanoke, Virginia, are shown dancing in a circle amid cornfields in a painting by John White. A 16th-century artist, White recorded the lives of mid-Atlantic tribes in a series of watercolors, renowned for their authenticity.

establish their first permanent settlements. Many tribes built villages along such major waterways as the Colorado River, the Mississippi River, the Ohio River, and the Tennessee River. Scholars estimate that the population of these villages sometimes reached as many as 30,000.

The rich soil of the river valleys they lived in provided Native Americans with the perfect environment in which to raise crops, and they proved expert farmers. Some tribes, such as the Cherokee, developed sophisticated techniques of agriculture that enabled them to grow a varied and abundant harvest each year. For example, they planted corn and beans together so that the nitrogen naturally produced by the beans fertilized the corn plants. In Cherokee society—as in most Native American communities—women took primary responsibility for farming, and men acted as fishermen and hunters.

In general, Native American tribes occupied a small territory, but some controlled acreage that extended for hundreds of square miles. The Iroquois, for example, were an Indian federation, at that time, composed of five separate tribes—the Cayuga, the Mohawk, the Oneida, the Onondaga, and the Seneca—which ruled a vast region that is now upstate New York. Just as the Iroquois federation included several different tribes, the Iroquoian linguistic family encompassed at least eight different tongues, spoken throughout eastern North America. The Iroquoian languages accounted for only a fraction of the hundreds of languages—and as many as 2,000 dialects—used by Native Americans.

The richness of Native American culture was reflected not only in the Indians' many languages but in the ceremonial rites they enacted; the beautiful pottery, baskets, and carvings they created; and the sophisticated creation myths they originated to explain their own origin. Yet despite the complexity of Native American culture, these people were viewed merely as savages by the Europeans who "discovered" North and South America in the late 15th and early 16th centuries.

The European Tide

In 1492, Christopher Columbus embarked on a voyage he hoped would lead him to the riches of the Indies (or India). During Columbus's era, mariners knew only one sure route to Asia. They sailed south, along the western coast of Africa, rounded the treacherous Cape of Good Hope—at Africa's southernmost tip—and headed east through the Indian Ocean. Columbus believed that a more direct course to the Orient lay toward the west and determined to test his theory for himself. He found sponsors for his voyage in Queen Isabella and King Ferdinand of Spain, a nation that led all others in the exploration of foreign lands.

Christopher Columbus arrives on the island of San Salvador, located in the Bahamas, in a watercolor by an unidentified artist dating from about 1800.

But Columbus proved to be wrong despite his careful nautical calculations. His journey led him not to Asia but to the Caribbean islands off the coast of North America. His discovery of a new continent—and of gold there—paved the way for scores of explorers from Italy (Columbus's native land) and Spain, including Vasco Núñez de Balboa, Francisco Vásquez de Coronado, Hernando Cortés, Juan Ponce de León, and Amerigo Vespucci (from whose name the word *America* was derived). During the 16th century, these men explored the continent and pushed farther into Central and South America, where they toppled the ancient empires of the Aztecs and Incas. But they enjoyed free run of the New World for less than 100 years.

In the latter part of the 16th century, settlers from northern Europe, primarily England, France, and the Netherlands, entered the race to acquire new territory and establish colonies abroad. In 1534, Frenchman Jacques Cartier led an expedition through "as fine a land as it is possible to see, being very fertile and covered with magnificent trees." The beautiful wilderness he described—which the French christened New France—is today the nation of Canada. In 1584, English explorer Sir Walter Raleigh staked claim to land along the mid-Atlantic coast of what was someday to be the United States. In honor of his nation's monarch, "The Virgin Queen," Elizabeth, he named the colony Virginia. And in 1609, Henry Hudson, a British navigator representing the Dutch East India Company, took possession of North American territory he named New Amsterdam, after the Dutch city of the same name.

Colonists Versus Indians

As the Europeans scrambled to found colonies, they met with the resistance of the native inhabitants of the New World, a people whom Columbus had mistakenly dubbed "Indians." The first contacts between Europeans and the Indians were not particularly hostile. Initially, they seemed to have greeted one another with mutual curiosity rather than aggression. If these travelers from an ocean away considered the Indians odd because they did not behave according to European customs, the Indians, for their part, found these shipborne visitors just as peculiar. Notwithstanding their differences, the two groups established trade relations.

As commerce got under way, more and more European settlements were established on the newly discovered landmass. With their muskets and gunpowder, the Europeans were able to overwhelm the eastern Woodland Indians and, later, the many tribes to the west. During the next two centuries, the European peoples would overrun North America and forcibly seize nearly all the Indians' territory. Although Native Americans felt a deep attachment to their land, they made no claims of private ownership. In their view, the land belonged to them no more than the moon or stars or sun did. In contrast, white settlers treated land as private property. They offered Indians money for their land. Although some among the tribes did sell their land to settlers, many refused to surrender territory they considered sacred. Then the settlers removed them by force of arms, ultimately relocating the majority of Native Americans to reservation lands in the West.

Indians and whites both shed much blood in violent conflicts over territory. In 1622, in Virginia, the Powhatan Confederacy launched an uprising that killed nearly one-third of the colony's white population. In 1637, in a clash with the Puritan settlers, the Pequot tribe, located in what is now eastern Connecticut, lost scores of its people. Decades later, the Wampanoag tribe waged a battle against New England settlers—a bloody encounter now called King Philip's War—that ended in defeat for the Indians in 1677. Continual skirmishes such as these set a pattern that lasted until the late 1800s, when a sprawling European civilization finished off the last Indian warriors.

More devastating, at first, than warfare for the Indians were the diseases the white men brought from

An engraving in History of the Discovery of America *depicts a battle between colonists and Native Americans in King Philip's War.*

Europe. Among these were not only the great killers such as smallpox and bubonic plague but also such diseases as measles, a virus from which most European sufferers eventually recovered. When an Indian contracted a European disease, his chances of survival were far less than those of an afflicted European because Native Americans lacked immunity to those scourges. Consequently, diseases carried by the Europeans ravaged Indian communities. Some scholars believe that these scourges reduced the Indian population by as much as 90 percent.

The Colonial Challenge

For many years after Columbus's discovery, a number of European nations struggled for control of North America. But only England could convince large numbers of its subjects to resettle across the Atlantic in order to develop and maintain permanent settlements overseas. By 1663 the British colony of New England could claim a population of about 40,000. In contrast, the French territory of New France was home to only 3,000 or so colonists.

Most French showed great reluctance to brave the bitter winters and rugged conditions of the colony. In addition, the economy of New France revolved around the trapping and selling of beaver and other animal pelts, and fur traders—the most influential members of the tiny community—discouraged the clearing and cultivation of the forests where they earned their living.

Although colonists were scarce in New France, clergy abounded. Jesuit priests flocked to the New World in order to seek converts to Roman Catholicism among the Native Americans there. In time these men of the cloth were second only to traders in the influence they wielded in New France. Jesuits enjoyed some success in spreading the doctrine of Christianity among Indians. But their mission work did not dramatically increase the overall number of Christians in the colony because as the priests won new Christians, they lost old ones. Many French traders abandoned their native faith after marrying Native American women—a practice common within New France.

Together the traders and Jesuit priests extended and strengthened France's hold on the colony, but by the mid-1700s French colonists in the New World were still outnumbered by the British at a ratio of about 20 to 1. This disadvantage in size ultimately cost the French their colony. In 1754 the British invaded New France during the French and Indian Wars, and the colonists there lacked the power to keep the redcoats at bay. By 1763, French colonial forces had been ousted from most of Canada.

The British expanded northward from the two colonies that composed their territory in North America: New England and Virginia. Although both these settlements shared a British colonial heritage, they differed dramatically in spirit. New England harbored religious refugees, such as Puritans, who founded colonies in what are now Massachusetts and Rhode Island, seeking the freedom to worship as they chose. In contrast, Virginia was home to people seeking economic opportunity rather than religious sanctuary.

Virginia began, in the words of one historian, as an "unsuccessful trading post" founded by the Virginia Company, a business enterprise based in London. The early Virginians were unable or unwilling to work to-

A Jesuit priest ministers to colonists in New France, as depicted in an etching from a late-17th-century history book.

Colonists trade firearms with an Indian leader in this frontispiece from a book about North America published in 1779.

gether to succeed economically or even to defend themselves against the Indians. Hostilities between whites and Native Americans—and among the colonists themselves—nearly destroyed the colony, which was weakened, too, by food shortages and epidemics of diseases such as smallpox. Virginians eventually turned their attention to farming rather than trade and grew tobacco for exportation. Many tobacco plantations also produced rice and indigo, a source of dye.

As tobacco agriculture spread throughout Virginia, which then included the future state of Maryland, the Virginia Company sought a reliable source of labor to till the fields and harvest the tobacco crop. At first they tried to enslave local Indians in order to use them as farm workers, but these efforts failed. Lacking enough laborers, the Virginia Company next attempted to entice Englishmen and Englishwomen to come to their colony. The company promised landholdings to merchants and mariners who would bring over more settlers. Those who accepted the offer came because they were poor and unwanted in their own country; colonization provided a means of escape from England. Many could not afford the cost of the trip overseas and so agreed to work on the plantations unpaid for four to seven years in exchange for having their passage financed by a wealthy planter. This arrangement was called indentured servitude. According to the terms of most agreements, indentured servants were free to work their own land after they had fulfilled their term of duty.

Despite the new influx of indentured servants and other settlers, the Virginia colony was verging on collapse. In 1624, England's king James I saw fit to intervene by declaring it a royal colony. Thus Virginia

A label from a London tobacco company bears the image of a Virginia colonist and a Native American.

NOVA BRITANNIA.

OFFERING MOST

Excellent fruites by Planting in
VIRGINIA.

Exciting all such as be well affected
to further the same.

LONDON
Printed for SAMVEL MACHAM, and are to befold at
his Shop in Pauls Church-yard, at the
Signe of the Bul-head.
1 6 0 9.

A page from a pamphlet,
published in London in 1609,
promotes immigration to
England's settlements in the
New World.

formally became an extension of England in the New World. Virginia's new status did little to diminish most British subjects' continued reliance on the contracts of indentured servitude as a means of immigrating to Virginia in the 17th century. Ties of nationality between planters and servants did little to better the rough lot of the latter, who were often worked to the brink of exhaustion. Physical cruelty was common, and overseers often beat laborers who failed to obey their orders. Because the servants claimed few legal rights, they were treated little better than actual slaves—their black counterparts in the colony.

The Trade in Slaves

The first African slaves were transported by ship to Virginia in 1619. They were probably brought ashore under the guise of being indentured servants because neither Virginia nor Maryland enacted laws regulating slavery until the 1660s. By the beginning of the 18th century, Virginians imported nearly 1,000 Africans a year into the colony. Most arrived in North America, in the words of one expert, "naked and in chains," having survived a brutal journey from Africa. Packed into the ship's compartment like fish in tins, they had no room to move. These slaves lived—and often died—where they lay, pinioned against their neighbor. As planters discovered the economic advantages of slavery, they turned to black slaves rather than white indentured servants as their main source of labor and thus perpetuated the Atlantic slave trade. The ready supply of slaves, in turn, aided the expansion of tobacco and cotton agriculture throughout the South.

The Puritan Heritage

In contrast to the South, the colonies of New England had little demand for slave labor and eventually became a center of the nation's antislavery movement. In fact, the first state to legally abolish slavery was Massachusetts, home to Puritans and Pilgrims—two groups that perhaps more than any others left their stamp on American culture. Puritans and Pilgrims arrived in North America at roughly the same time but established separate settlements and held different philosophies.

The Puritans, originally from the region in England known as East Anglia, sought religious freedom for themselves but not necessarily for others. They followed the teachings of the 16th-century Protestant reformer John Calvin and applied them to the Anglican church, or Church of England. Puritans championed a purification of the Anglican church, which they believed was controlled by power-hungry bishops. They urged the reorganization of church structure so that no single member of the clergy rose above the rank of parish priest.

The Pilgrims, in contrast to the Puritans, had abandoned all hope of reforming the Church of England to their satisfaction. Instead of trying to change the church from within, they left it to form their own separate religious movement. In splitting off from the church, the separatists provoked the suspicion and hostility of church fathers and of the British crown, which harassed them until they fled England. In 1609 the Pilgrims sought refuge in the Dutch city of Leiden, but within a decade they decided to make their home in America. In 1620 they boarded the ship *Mayflower* and set out for the New World.

The Pilgrims put down roots in Plymouth, Massachusetts, and suffered through several brutal winters, the first of which deprived them of nearly half their party. After 10 years in the New World, the colony of New Plymouth claimed only 300 members. The Pilgrims were vastly outnumbered by the Puritan settlements—such as Boston—that sprang up along Massachusetts Bay. In 1630, John Winthrop sailed to Massachusetts accompanied by about 1,000 fellow Puri-

A portrait of Puritan leader John Winthrop.

tans. Winthrop and his followers formed the Massachusetts Bay Company, for which he served as the first colonial governor. Building upon the doctrines of John Calvin, Winthrop tried to create a government guided by principles of Christianity as he saw them. For slightly more than a decade, he proved an effective leader of the New England Puritans, or Congregationalists, as they came to be known in America.

The attempt to establish a religious state was not well received by settlers of other Protestant denominations, whose personal liberties were frequently obstructed by Puritan religious authorities. Until about 1690 the Congregationalists were often ruthlessly intolerant of non-Puritan groups, to whom they denied the right to vote within the colony. Puritans not only discriminated against Christians outside their ranks, they also persecuted them—even hanging Quakers who tried to preach in the town of Boston. Their refusal to rec-

A Quaker farm in Bucks County, Pennsylvania, as depicted by American painter Edward Hicks. Many Quakers sought refuge in the state founded by their coreligionist William Penn in 1681.

ognize other religious points of view frightened many potential settlers away from the Boston area.

Although the Puritans ceased coming to the colonies in large numbers after the 1640s, they continued to influence the course of American culture for many years. The Puritan founders of New England prized education and individual accomplishment and took great pride in their native language—English. They introduced to the New World English traditions of law and government that served as a model for the legal system and constitution of the United States. In addition, Puritans formed the basis of an American creed that mingled piety and practicality: They believed that people best served God by working hard, saving their money, and achieving success in business. Future immigrants to America would be expected to adopt many values rooted in Puritanism as part of the process of becoming American.

The Immigrant Groups of the Eighteenth Century

During the 1600s, the English founded and dominated the colonies both in Virginia and Massachusetts. But the 1700s ushered in a new era in immigration to America as Jewish, Scotch-Irish, German, Huguenot (French Protestant), Scottish, and Welsh emigrants all converged on the colonies. The ethnic diversity that distinguishes the United States and Canada first appeared not in New England—where nearly everyone shared a British heritage—but in the mid-Atlantic regions of New York, Pennsylvania, and Delaware. As early as 1643, a French priest remarked that he heard 17 languages spoken in the streets of the Dutch settlement of New Amsterdam. (This observation is especially surprising because only several hundred people lived in the city at that time.)

Because few of their own citizens were interested in settling in New Netherland, the Dutch welcomed im-

German Jews erected the Beth Elohim Synagogue in Charleston, South Carolina, in 1794. The building was destroyed by fire in 1838.

migrants of all religions and nationalities, including Jews. In 1654, the colonies' first Jews—23 in all—arrived at the port of New Amsterdam after sailing from Brazil, from which they had been expelled. The small Jewish population of colonial America spread north into Rhode Island—where they established the Touro Synagogue in Newport in about 1763—and south into the Carolinas. Although they were a tiny minority, Jews participated energetically in the life of the colonies: Haym Salomon, a Polish-born Jew, helped finance the American Revolution, and after the United States had achieved its independence, Uriah Phillips Levy rose to the rank of commodore in the U.S. Navy. Despite their contributions, Jews were forbidden from voting or holding office within many of the colonies until the ratification of the U.S. Constitution, which ensures in Article VI that "no religious test shall ever be required as a qualification to any office or public trust."

The Scotch-Irish

Jewish Americans brought their unique traditions into the colonies, but they did not change the complexion of North America as dramatically as did the Scotch-Irish, one of the largest non-English immigrant groups in North America. The Scotch-Irish originally lived in Scotland but had resettled in Ulster (Northern Ireland) early in the 17th century. They were brought there by the English to act as a buffer between the Catholic natives of Ireland and England's occupying forces in the region. Thus, the Scotch-Irish found themselves continually embroiled in the bloody conflicts that plagued Northern Ireland.

Even without the ongoing threat of violence, the Scotch-Irish could barely eke out a living in Ulster—a region of Ireland that, like all others, was plagued by poor economic conditions. After 1717, a combination of ruined crops, high rents, and religious persecution drove them to seek a livelihood away from British and Irish shores. Many Scotch-Irish believed that their salvation from poverty lay across the ocean in North America. Too poor to emigrate on their own, many entered into indentured servitude and thus made their way to the New World.

Once they had fulfilled their term as indentured servants, many Scotch-Irish headed for Pennsylvania, a colony that had been founded by the Quaker leader William Penn as a haven for persecuted Quakers. Established in 1681, Pennsylvania welcomed not only Quakers but immigrants of many religious faiths and nationalities. During the colonial era, as many as 250,000 Scotch-Irish settled there, grateful for the opportunity to farm their own land and the freedom to practice Presbyterianism, the branch of Protestantism to which most Scotch-Irish belonged. So many Scotch-Irish flocked to Pennsylvania that the choicest farmland there quickly became scarce, and those not among the very first arrivals soon overflowed into southern territory, including the backcountry of the Carolinas and Virginia.

The Scotch-Irish made a strong imprint on American society, especially in the field of politics. The 56 signers of the Declaration of Independence included 14 Scotch-Irishmen, and men of Scotch-Irish descent have served their country in government since the earliest days of the republic, especially in the office of the presidency. The 11 Scotch-Irish presidents of the United States include James K. Polk (1845–49), James Buchanan (1857–61), Andrew Jackson (1829–37), Andrew Johnson (1865–69), Ulysses S. Grant (1869–77), Chester A. Arthur (1881–85), Grover Cleveland (1885–89 and 1893–97), William Henry Harrison (1841), Benjamin Harrison (1889–93), William McKinley (1897–1901), and Woodrow Wilson (1913–21).

From Germany and France

Like the Scotch-Irish, German immigrants to North America, most of whom arrived after about 1720, tended to make their homes in Pennsylvania. Although the vast majority of Germans remained there, some moved east to New York—gathering along the banks of the Hudson River—and south to colonies such as Virginia. Wherever they settled, the Germans—many of whom belonged to the persecuted Mennonite, Moravian, and Dunkard sects of Protestantism—encountered a mixed response. On the one hand, colonists of longer standing praised the Germans for their skill at house building and farming and their seemingly endless capacity for hard work. On the other hand, more established Americans mocked the Germans, claiming that they cared more for their barns and livestock than for their children.

The Germans' critics also condemned them for being clannish and rebuked their seeming unwillingness to learn the language and customs of the English majority. The statesman and diplomat Benjamin Franklin, for example, warned that the Germans swarming into Pennsylvania would "Germanize" the other settlers. In a sense his fears were justified, because Germans eventually claimed more descendants than any other ethnic group in America. In fact, by 1986, according to the U.S. Census Bureau, the leading ancestral background of America's residents was no longer British but German. Roughly 44 million U.S. citizens, or 18 percent of the populace, claimed total or partial German heritage, a few hundred thousand more than claimed British descent.

Although 18th-century German immigrants aroused hostility at times, they received little of the hatred Protestant colonists reserved for Roman Catholics of all national origins. Most Protestants harbored a fear and loathing of Catholicism ingrained in them as children, and they violently objected to the presence of Catholics in America. In reality, only a small number of European Catholics immigrated to the colonies—most choosing Maryland as their home—but they immediately faced a tangle of laws that denied them the rights enjoyed by Protestants within the colonies. For example, legal restrictions banned Catholics from voting and worshiping in many settlements. Not until the American Revolution did Catholics win full civil rights.

In Canada, the order of discrimination between Protestants and Catholics was reversed. Catholic colonists in New France—although desperate for immigrants from their native land—shut Canada's doors to Huguenots. Huguenots began their exodus from France in 1685, when King Louis XIV stripped the Huguenots of all their political power by revoking the Edict of

In 1680 William Penn received the charter for Pennsylvania from King Charles II of England. Penn recruited hundreds of Europeans to the New World by printing pamphlets in English, German, French, and Dutch describing the wonders of Pennsylvania.

A painting depicts Huguenots, or French Protestants, after the revocation of the Edict of Nantes in 1685. Huguenot families quickly rose to prominence within the colonies and wielded influence out of proportion to their small number.

Nantes, a document that had afforded these Calvinists religious and political freedom in Catholic France. Banned from the French colony in North America, most immigrant Huguenots journeyed instead to British strongholds in Charleston, South Carolina, and New York City.

Huguenots as a group were fairly wealthy, and they quickly achieved economic success in the colonies, some earning fortunes as merchants in the port cities of America. Although they organized their own French-speaking churches rather than join those of Anglo-Saxon Protestants, Huguenots ultimately preserved few ties with their native culture. They quickly learned English and within a generation or two many intermarried with English families and joined the Church of England.

The Jews, Scotch-Irish, Germans, and Huguenots represented but a few of the newcomers who altered the face of 18th-century America. These groups, and other western European immigrants, stand as the most noteworthy of 18th-century immigrant groups, in part because English immigration had greatly diminished in the late 17th century. After about 1660 the British government—fearing a wholesale exodus of English laborers to North America—discouraged emigration from England. Even so, as late as the 1770s, skilled workers from England, Scotland, and Wales continued to find their way to America. Their number was increased by another sector of Britain's population, criminals, who were shipped to America against their will. British authorities banished some 50,000 lawbreakers to the New World rather than further overcrowd the country's teeming prisons. Most colonists objected to this policy but had no choice but to accept it until the British grip on the colonies was broken by the American War of Independence.

Canada's Story

Canada's ethnic composition was somewhat different from that of its neighbor to the south. Before the British seized Canada from the French, the vast majority of New France's 60,000 settlers claimed French origin. Most lived around the two major Canadian cities of Quebec and Montreal—a veritable metropolis with nearly 9,000 inhabitants—or along the shores of the St. Lawrence River.

Because Britain coveted Canada as a part of its empire, the crown continually tried to strengthen its hold on the region. Hence, the British eagerly welcomed their supporters'—including Scots, Quakers, and Mennonites—fleeing the United States at the end of the American Revolution. The British gave their partisans, called Loyalists, many incentives to relocate to Canada. They rewarded newcomers from the colonies with landholdings and exempted Quakers and Mennonites from military service, opposed on principle by both religions.

Blacks, too, benefited from the policies of the Canadian government. In 1833, Britain abolished slavery within its empire, including its holdings in the Western Hemisphere: Canada and the British West Indies—the Caribbean islands of Jamaica, the Bahamas, the Caymans, the British Virgin Islands, Leeward Islands, Windward Islands, Trinidad, and Tobago. It would be 32 years before the United States followed suit and outlawed slavery within the nation by ratifying the Thir-

British troops land at the base of the Plains of Abraham, just outside Quebec, in June 1759. The British victory there was a turning point in the battle for New France.

teenth Amendment to the U.S. Constitution. During that period (1833–65), American slaves, seeking liberty, streamed north across the border into Canada. Canadian antislavery organizations aided these refugees, as did American abolitionists, who established the "Underground Railroad," which provided renegade slaves with safe quarters along their route to freedom. When the American Civil War broke out, blacks began returning to the United States, some to take part in the "War to End Slavery." Just as Canada's black population had once swelled, it now shrank and ultimately remained small.

More numerous than blacks were the thousands of immigrants—mostly from the British Isles—who poured into Canada during the first century of British rule. By the 1860s settlers from the British Isles outnumbered the French by a two-to-one margin. Nevertheless, Canada went on to become a nation that accommodates both languages and cultures.

An Evolving Identity

By the time of the American Revolution, distinct patterns of population had emerged within the colonies, which had grown from about 200,000 inhabitants in 1690 to about 2.5 million in the 1770s. In New England the descendants of the original Puritan and Pilgrim settlers formed the overwhelming majority. The next largest groups were the Scotch-Irish and the Welsh. The Middle Atlantic states contained more national diversity. Pennsylvania, for example, was composed of about 33 percent Germans and nearly 40 percent Scotch and Scotch-Irish. In New York, Virginia, North Carolina, and South Carolina, more than 50 percent of the inhabitants were from other than English ancestry. In spite of this diversity, prerevolutionary colonists conceived of themselves as part of the British Empire and viewed English manners and mores as an ideal to which many tried to conform. But as the colonists moved to-

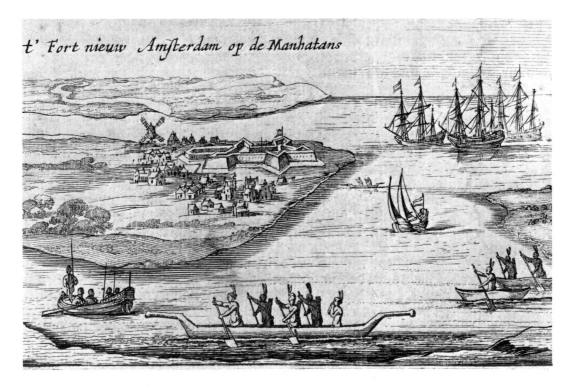

t' Fort nieuw Amsterdam op de Manhatans

ward self-government, many began to think of themselves as Americans, a unique people, who stood as a model of liberty throughout the world. Of course, not all inhabitants of the United States—namely, Afro-Americans and Native Americans—shared in the fruits of independence. Nevertheless, the name America evoked a vision of liberty—political, religious, and economic—to millions across the globe who saw in the United States a place of opportunity lacking in their own lands. After 1830 they began a massive immigration to the United States that changed the ethnic composition of the American people in fundamental ways.

A view of New Amsterdam in about 1626, when it was still part of the Dutch colony of New Netherlands. In 1664 the English wrested the settlement from Dutch control and renamed it New York.

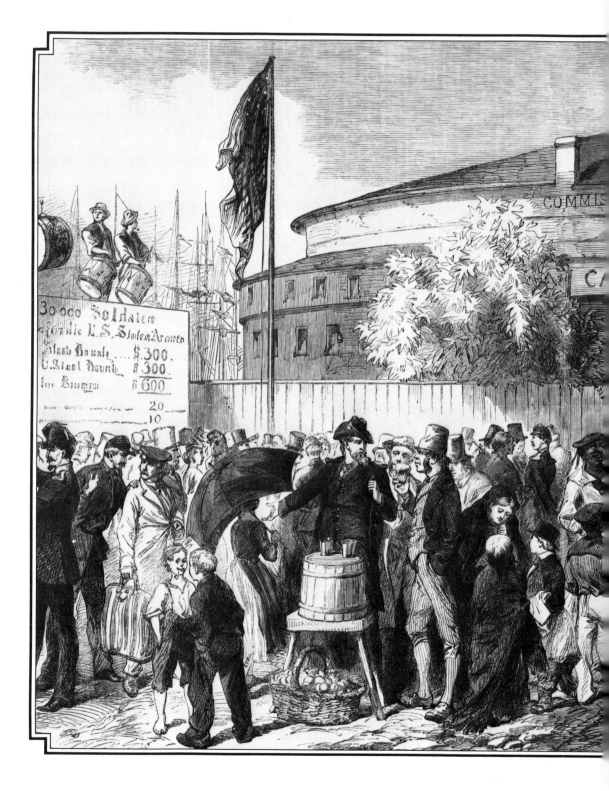

Union soldiers recruit newly arrived Irish and German immigrants at the Castle Garden immigration station in 1864.

Setting the Stage for Immigration

When America's Founding Fathers drafted the U.S. Constitution, they failed to make any provision for Congress to regulate immigration. However, the federal government legislated the process whereby foreigners could become U.S. citizens. In 1790, Congress passed a law providing guidelines for naturalization (the legal process whereby aliens become citizens). The legislation required that an applicant for citizenship be a "free white person" who had lived in the United States for two years. In 1801 the administration of President Thomas Jefferson broadened the residency requirement from two to five years. The five-year law has remained on the books ever since.

Except for naturalization, Congress permitted the states to enact and enforce their own immigration statutes, just as the colonies once had. New York—the nation's chief port of entry by the 1820s—served as the model for all other states in its innovative legislation and programs for new immigrants. By the middle of the 19th century, about two-thirds of all immigrants passed through New York City. The city's position as a leading port for both commercial and passenger ships was reinforced in 1825 with the opening of the Erie Canal, a historic waterway that provided a route between the Atlantic Ocean and the Great Lakes. In addition, railroad companies made New York a hub of transportation by offering train service from New York to the far-flung western towns that marked many immigrants' final destination.

At first, New York's legislation was in the service of screening out paupers and those with communicable diseases. For example, in 1824 the state passed a law requiring that ship captains post bonds as security against any possible expenses that paupers—brought into port by the captains—might incur. As the number of immigrants grew during the 19th century, so, too, did the scope and design of New York's legislation. Lawmakers, who at first wanted only to shield the state from the financial drain caused by penniless immigrants, soon shifted their focus to the protection of the immigrants themselves. In 1855, New York's State Board of Commissioners of Immigration opened Castle Garden, a reception center for immigrants. Officials at Castle Garden provided baths, food staples, and lodging for those just off the boat.

The dangers of Castle Garden are dramatized in this etching, which shows a thief rummaging through the contents of a woman's purse.

In addition, Castle Garden authorities protected "greenhorns" from the many con artists who preyed on vulnerable and confused new arrivals. Some "runners," as these fraudulent men were called, grabbed immigrants' baggage and checked them into overpriced boardinghouses in exchange for a kickback from the owners. Runners even sold the greenhorns phony tickets on steamboats and railroads. Castle Garden officials attempted to eliminate these abuses by providing information about decent boardinghouses and arranging transportation west. In 1892, Ellis Island—a 27-acre compound located just off the island of Manhattan—replaced Castle Garden as the chief entry station of immigrants to the United States and continued to serve that function until 1943.

From Sailboat to Steamship

Government authorities aided immigrants even before they reached dry land by legislating the conditions aboard the ships carrying them to the New World. Many of the intolerable conditions experienced by 19th-century immigrants had remained unchanged since the colonial era. During the 16th and 17th centuries, voyages to North America sometimes lasted as long as two months. Immigrants were herded into dank steerage holds where they breathed fetid air and ate rotting food. Diseases spread like wildfire under such unwholesome conditions, and, in addition, immigrants often had to withstand abusive treatment from the ship's crew. Particularly shocking was an incident aboard a ship bound for Pennsylvania in 1752. After setting out from Holland with 340 passengers, the ship reached its destination with only 21 still alive. Some of these hardships continued well into the 19th century, and many immigrants would always remember their passage to North America as a nightmare. One woman from Germany recalled the following:

A 19th-century English shipping line advertises passage between Liverpool and Boston.

We left from Germany . . . and all the children got measles. Some of them died and they threw them into the water like cattle. It was a pathetic thing that . . . I will never forget. And you can imagine how the women carried on. They took a child away from them and they just tossed it in, nice and quiet.

Advances in maritime technology gradually improved the conditions on board immigrant-bearing ships. In 1819 the first steam-powered ship—an invention of American engineer Robert Fulton—crossed the Atlantic Ocean. Steamships shortened the length of the average voyage from eight weeks to just one. They also made the journey to America more affordable and offered passengers cleaner and more airy accommodations.

Steamships altered the conditions of passage to North America, but they ultimately changed much more than that. During the age of the sailboat, immigrants had journeyed to America on commercial vessels, which carried them as extra cargo. Therefore, the process of immigration was tied directly to trade routes. Thus, Europeans could immigrate to America only if their homeland was one that engaged in transatlantic commerce in North America. Similarly, their destination was never one of their own choosing but instead marked the starting (or end) point in the cycle of trade.

Steamships revolutionized the means of immigration because they so drastically shortened the length of the voyage. For the first time people could reasonably expect to survive the passage overseas, and scores of Europeans, who had previously refused to make the journey, now were willing to give it a try. For their part, the steamship companies realized that a fortune lay in the transporting of millions of immigrants to America. They began to view immigration as a profitable commercial venture in its own right and carried emigrants from all across Europe to the New World. According to historian Thomas Sowell: "Steam-powered ships caused a drastic change in the origins of immigrants to

America. In the era of wind-driven ships, European immigrants came almost exclusively from northern and western Europe. With the advent of steam-powered ships, suddenly immigration was overwhelmingly from southern and eastern Europe."

Steerage passengers aboard a steamship demand a meal from a dishonest cook. Although passengers were guaranteed food with the price of their ticket, they often had to pay extra for basic provisions during their voyage.

Leaving Home

In the century and a half after the end of the Napoleonic Wars in 1815, over 60 million Europeans sought a new life elsewhere. What forced so many millions out of the Old World? Scholars have offered various explanations for the dramatic transformation of Europe during the the late 18th and early 19th centuries. Historian Eugene Weber cites a "shift from stability to mobility" as the underlying force of the age. In *Europe Since 1715* he writes:

One cannot deny the number or importance of the changes and convulsions of this time. They led from absolute monarchies to constitutions and republics . . . from political passivity to . . . participation and reform, from the speed and productivity of men and beasts to that of machines, from cottage industries [textile manufacturing such as weaving performed by peasant women at home] to great manufacturing hives in factories and cities.

Of all these changes, however, perhaps the most important was a boom in Europe's population. Between 1750 and 1850 the population of the Continent rose from about 140 million to about 260 million, and by the time of the First World War, to almost 400 million.

The number of people in Europe increased, but the amount of land remained the same. Thus, peasants who had expected to subsist on the land found themselves either entirely landless or with too small a plot to farm productively. Unable to survive as farmers, millions migrated to the cities in search of work. Although the newly developing industrial centers employed many surplus rural laborers, they could not provide work for all. Consequently, millions found themselves with the choice of either starving at home or immigrating to other places where opportunities for work were more plentiful. In two-thirds of all cases this meant going to the United States and Canada, but more than 30 percent of immigrants relocated to Africa, Australia, and South America—in particular to Brazil and Argentina.

An etching from the December 22, 1849, edition of the Illustrated London News *shows impoverished Irish receiving a handout of clothing during the potato famine. Food and land shortages in Europe acted to spur immigration throughout the 19th century.*

The Lure of the New World

There were as many reasons for wanting to come to North America, particularly the United States, as there were for leaving Europe. After the War of 1812—a three-year armed conflict between the United States and Great Britain that ended in 1815—the young republic enjoyed a period of rapid economic growth. The cotton industry boomed in the South—spreading from the Eastern Seaboard to the Gulf states of Texas, Louisiana, Alabama, and Mississippi—and in the North trade and industry blossomed. Suddenly mines and factories clamored for a steady supply of cheap labor; railroad companies needed workers to lay thousands of miles of tracks across America. Cities, too, grew by leaps and bounds: New York City—which reigned not only as the nation's major port but also as an important manufacturing center—had over 800,000 residents in 1860, compared to only 20,000 or so at the time of the American Revolution.

During the early 19th century, the West, too, received a stream of energetic newcomers ready to build new lives in rough terrain. Immigrants in search of land traveled by train and canal boat to the virgin wilderness and prairies of the Midwest. They typically began their trek westward by traveling up the Hudson River to Albany, following the Erie Canal to Buffalo, New York, and then taking another boat, train, or wagon to Michigan, Missouri, Wisconsin, Minnesota, or one of the other western territories. After the land shortages of Europe, America seemed to these pioneers a boundless land, with prosperity for all who were willing to clear and till their own land.

Just as William Penn had tried to attract settlers for his colony, western states sought to entice Europeans in the 19th century. States attracted pioneers by setting up special bureaus of immigration and sending to Europe reams of propaganda about the United States. Some states even hired agents who spoke foreign languages to travel to America's port cities and inform immigrants just off the boat about the many opportunities available in a particular state. In 1845, Michigan became the first state to maintain an agent for recruitment in New York, and then other states quickly followed that example. States also advertised for new settlers in foreign newspapers. From reading the material one would never know that Minnesota had winter or that it took hard labor and some capital to begin a farm from scratch. In 1862, Congress gave a boost to the West's recruitment efforts by passing the Homestead Act, which gave many landless people in the United States hope of acquiring western property. This law awarded 160 acres for a nominal fee to anyone who settled and cultivated unoccupied lots for at least 5 years.

The U.S. government hastened the settlement of the West, too, by promising the railroads tracts of public land on which to build their lines. Once the tracks had been laid and a route established, land values along the railroad skyrocketed. The companies helped defray their construction costs by selling this property to immigrant pioneers. In 1854 the Illinois Central became the first railroad to recruit immigrants, and after the Civil War other companies followed suit. They offered free transportation to bring people west and easy terms for the purchase of land. The Northern Pacific Railroad even published newspapers in Germany and from 1882 to 1883 distributed over 600,000 copies of its publications in 6 foreign languages.

Although thousands of people profited from the expansion of the railroads, an equal number suffered—namely, Native Americans. In truth, the acreage lavished on the railroads by the U.S. government was often the rightful property of Indian tribes. Native Americans fought white encroachment on their land both through the courts and in face-to-face confrontations. But in the end they were overpowered by white settlers, who had the backing of the entire U.S. Army. Too often the conflict between Indian and white interests ended in

tragedy for Native Americans. No tribal history dramatized the plight of Native Americans more poignantly than that of the Cherokee. In the winter of 1838–39 the Cherokee were forcibly removed from their ancestral lands in the southeastern United States and sent on a forced migration to a reservation in Oklahoma. This journey came to be known as the Trail of Tears because of the Cherokee's suffering. Between one-fourth and one-half of them died before reaching their new home in the West.

Newcomers were encouraged to migrate not only by states and railroads but by the steamship companies that brought them to the United States. Steamship lines employed thousands of agents to sell tickets and inform prospective immigrants of the advantages of their lines and about the quality of life in the United States. In European port cities, steamship companies provided dormitories in which immigrants could spend the night before embarking on their journey. The companies would also delouse immigrants in order to prevent an outbreak of vermin—often carriers of disease—aboard ship.

As important as all these activities were, just as significant were the letters sent home by those who had gone before. Those who settled first wrote to their fam-

A construction crew from the Northern Pacific Railroad Company poses alongside a locomotive in 1885.

Steamship lines often sold tickets to more passengers than could comfortably fit on board. The boat pictured here carried more than 2,300 immigrants on a voyage from the Russian port of Batumi to Canada.

ilies and friends in Europe describing the manifold blessings of America. Many complained, but most declared that people in the United States lived vastly better than those in the Old World. Eager readers passed the letters—some of which contained steamship tickets or money to purchase passage—from hand to hand and village to village in Europe and even published them in the local newspapers. These messages created a virtual "American fever," especially in the Scandinavian countries.

But accuracy in these letters mattered less than conveying a good impression to worried relatives in the homeland. Many letters gave exaggerated descriptions of a land of milk and honey. As a result, the settlers who followed the first waves of adventurers often received a rude awakening when they stepped off the boat. "We often find that he who . . . describes the beautiful carriage he owns is the owner of a wheelbarrow for which he himself serves as the locomotive," wrote one disappointed arrival.

The Sixty Million

Given the conditions in Europe and the attractions of the New World, it is no wonder that millions left their homes to begin life anew. The different groups that came fell into three categories. The "old immigrants," from northern and western Europe—mostly Irish, Germans, and Scandinavians—arrived before about 1880. This first great wave from Europe coincided with two simultaneous 19th-century migrations: one from China, the other from Canada. The next great surge of immigration started in about 1880 and lasted until approximately 1920. This second wave consisted of emigrants from southern and eastern Europe—Italians and Jews— and also Japanese. The third and most recent immigration is composed of the ethnic groups arriving in the United States since World War II.

The flow to Canada from Europe was considerably less than that to the United States. But Irish fleeing the potato famine of the 1840s, as well as many Scots, English, and Welsh from the British Isles, sought new life there. In the 1830s, Canadian immigration averaged about 27,000 annually. With economic expansion, it gradually grew but did not exceed 60,000 yearly until the 1880s. Immigration topped 100,000 annually 3 times during the 1880s. In the late 19th century many Germans and Scandinavians settled on the western Canadian prairies.

All of these newcomers contributed much to the economic expansion of American society. Because they did not always share the same values as colonial Americans, they also can claim responsibility for the development of American culture and the making of a diverse nation. Perhaps no group so enriched the new republic as did the Irish. According to one expert: "Irish Americans introduced an ingredient so vital to American life that today we take it for granted—cultural diversity." Thus, Irish Americans paved the way for a generation of emigrants from Europe—men and women who would change the face of the United States.

A photograph dating from 1900 shows Irish women at work as waitresses in Child's Restaurant in New York City.

THE OLD IMMIGRANTS

The 3.5 million Irish who landed on American shores in 1830–90 arrived from a land with a rich cultural history and a poor economic one. Beginning in the 12th century, England—a neighboring country lying just to the west—invaded Ireland and subjugated its people. Although the Irish fought valiantly against military occupation by the British, they lived for centuries under the thumb of oppressive colonial rule. In the 16th century England's king Henry VIII broke with the Catholic church, and England became a Protestant nation. Thus, beginning in the 1500s, the enmity between the English and Irish was aggravated by differences in religion as well as nationality. Protestant English enforced a series of punitive statutes designed to impoverish the Irish people, the vast majority of whom were Catholic. One of these laws, for example, mandated that when a Catholic farmer died, his land must be partitioned among his descendants. After a few generations of these divisions, family tracts of land became so small that they were hardly worth owning.

On their plots, the Irish grew potato plants—the one staple of their diet. The destruction of the potato crop by a fungus at the end of the 1840s ushered in the "Potato Famine." With neither food nor economic aid from Britain, Irishmen and Irishwomen died by the

Irish leave Dublin's seaport for Liverpool, England, aboard the steamships Nimrod *and* Athlone.

tens of thousands during the famine; estimates run as high as 1.5 million deaths. Historian Hasia R. Diner described Ireland during the Potato Famine as "a country of starving and homeless paupers. It was noticed that the skin of starving human beings became rough to the touch, very dry like parchment. The shoulder blades were thrown up high. The hair became thin on the head. . . . Sores grew between the fingers."

The only hope for survival lay in escape from Ireland. Those with any funds at all generally chose one of two destinations: Liverpool, England—one of Great Britain's largest industrial and manufacturing centers—or North America. The journey to Liverpool, just across the Irish Sea from Dublin, took only a single day by ferry. But the English were unenthusiastic about the growing number of Irish entering port cities such as Liverpool and therefore encouraged the refugees to head for North America. During the 1840s and 1850s, millions chose this option and set out across the Atlantic. These wretched people were so weak that many fell to disease either at sea or soon after their arrival in North America. In 1847 the British government reported that 89,738 Irish had embarked for Canada and that 5,293 had died at sea and another 10,037 had died in hospitals or under quarantine within a short time of their arrival. Mortality rates for emigrants bound for the United States were scarcely better.

Work Force of the Nation

So many of the Irish were destitute when they landed that they did not even have enough funds to leave port cities. Hence, Boston and New York became the home of many Irish, as did Montreal in Canada. In the port cities, the Irish easily found employment. Little skill or education was required to work as stevedores—unloading and loading ships on the docks—or to dig up crumbling streets and build new ones.

Nor did the Irishmen have difficulty finding unskilled jobs in the nation's rapidly growing transportation system. Three thousand miles of canals were built before the Civil War, along with 30,000 miles of railroad track. What was needed was a strong back and willingness to work for a dollar a day. The Irish qualified on both counts. Their labor built the Illinois Central Railroad connecting Chicago and New Orleans, and later, along with the Chinese, they helped lay the tracks for the Union Pacific Railroad.

Because the Irish found jobs along the transportation routes, Irish enclaves appeared throughout the United States, often close to the railroads. By the end of the 19th century, Irish communities were well established in new locales such as San Francisco and New Orleans. The largest concentrations of Irish, however, were in New York, Massachusetts, Pennsylvania, and Illinois. These states contained more than half the total Irish-American population.

Erin's Daughters

Irishmen held railway and construction jobs, but it was the Irishwomen who served as the main force within their community. Unlike other immigrant groups of the 19th century, the Irish were composed of a female majority. In Ireland women had often postponed marriage and worked out of economic necessity. Hence, many young Irishwomen had the freedom and funds to make the journey to the New World. Once in America, Irishwomen repeated the pattern and remained single longer than women from any other immigrant group. These young women frequently found employment as domestics, an occupation shunned by many other ethnic groups. In fact, the figure of the obstinate Irish maid—"Bridget" or "Nora"—became an ethnic stereotype that lingered well into the 20th century.

Historian Hasia Diner has described marriages among impoverished Irish Americans as stormy and short lived. Irish families sometimes suffered from violence and desertion on the part of husbands and fathers. In her book *Erin's Daughters in America*, published in 1983, Diner writes, "An Irish immigrant woman who chose in the 1860s or 1870s to marry a construction worker in Boston or Providence or a factory hand living in New York or Worcester [Massachusetts] ran a very high risk of having someday to be sole support for a house full of children, existing indeed on starvation's edge." For these reasons, Irishwomen often remained single for years, and once married, they often headed single-parent households. In 1870, in Philadelphia, 16.9

In the early 20th century the Kirkman Company promoted its Borax soap with an advertising campaign featuring the "endorsement" of Irish washerwomen.

percent of Irishwomen headed families compared to only 5.9 percent of German females. Only blacks had a higher rate of female-headed families.

Two young workers in a textile factory pose by their mechanical loom.

Tenement Life

Even when women and children both worked, family income was often insufficient for adequate housing and a healthful diet. In Boston, one historian tells us, the Irish lived in "crammed hovels" without furniture and with patches of "dirty straw" for bedding. In New York City, Irish families lived in the city's worst, overcrowded slums. Under such conditions it is no wonder that Irish neighborhoods were plagued with diseases like typhoid, typhus, and cholera. Not until after the Civil War did public-health programs gain wide acceptance in the United States and improve the living conditions of immigrants.

The most unfortunate Irish immigrants became so destitute that they had no place to go but the public poorhouses or lunatic asylums. In New York City, in the 1850s, 85 percent of the foreign-born admitted to Bellevue Hospital had Irish names, and most admissions to Blackwell's Island, the city's asylum for the insane, were also Irish.

With the passage of time, however, Irish Americans moved out of poverty, into better jobs and improved housing. This was a slow process, and frequently the second generation lived only marginally better than the first. First-generation Irishwomen put behind them the drudgery performed by their mothers either in domestic service or in New England textile firms—many located in the town of Lowell, Massachusetts—where they worked on mechanized looms and spinning machines. Irishwomen born in America often took advantage of the public education available to them and became teachers, nurses, and public employees. In the 1880s they made up a quarter of Boston's and New York's teachers, and by the early 20th century these women made up significant proportions of the teachers in urban schools across America.

The Public Life

Irishmen, too, progressed, many rising to prominence in their community through local politics. The Irish arrived in the United States at a time when the political process was becoming more democratic. By 1840 nearly every white male in the United States—rich or poor—could cast his ballot in elections. In the words of one expert: "[t]he gentry yielded to professional politicians who viewed party management as a vocation." The Irish quickly joined the ranks of these "party managers," who wielded enormous influence within the Democratic party.

By the end of the century, Irish "bosses" were controlling ward politics in cities with sizable Irish populations, such as Boston and New York and, later, Jersey City and Chicago. In an era devoid of social services for the poor, ward bosses acted as one-man charitable institutions. They raised funds for christenings and funerals, provided financial assistance to impoverished widows, and did innumerable favors for people who continuously lived on the brink of eviction or starvation. In return, the grateful populace turned out for every election and cast their ballot as they were told.

Under this system—which lasted well into the 20th century—Irishmen won mayoral elections across the nation. Boss Frank Hague of Jersey City held the office of mayor for three decades, from 1917 to 1947, and Mayor Richard Daley of Chicago, the last of the big-city bosses, reigned over the Windy City from 1955 to 1970. Many of these figures became mythologized in the history of American politics, none more so than Boston mayor James Michael Curley, who once won office while in jail. Once in power, the Irish politicians used their power to hire Irish policemen, firemen, and civil servants. City halls operating under the rule of Irishmen often awarded construction contracts to Irish firms. The political system thus became an important institution of social mobility for the American Irish.

Irish-American politicians amassed enormous power in urban centers, but they fared worse when running for national office. In 1928, Al Smith, who rose through New York City politics to the governorship of the state, made a bid for the presidency. The voters rejected Smith, in part because of his Catholicism, and not until the election of John F. Kennedy in 1960 was a Catholic voted into the nation's top office.

As important as politics was for Irish Americans, the Catholic church was no less so. The church in Ireland had been a bulwark of strength against English oppression. When the Irish encountered similar hostility to their religious beliefs in Protestant America, the church again proved itself to be a source of spiritual comfort. French and native-born priests controlled the

Frank Hague, longtime mayor of Jersey City, New Jersey, poses for the press with his wife.

Boston mayor John F. Fitzgerald—popularly known as Honey Fitz—throws out the first ball of the 1912 World Series.

American Catholic church when the Irish arrived in large numbers, but the Irish quickly moved up, becoming priests, nuns, and archbishops and leaders in the church. Archbishop John Hughes of New York in the 1840s was the first of many Irish spokesmen in the Catholic church.

The twin pillars of politics and religion helped the Irish overcome the bitter poverty they faced in the mid-1800s. As of 1980, the nearly 20 million Americans of Irish descent were more likely than their fellow citizens to be professionals and managers. Irish Americans had also earned the admiration of other Americans through a series of remarkable contributions to the cultural life of the United States. The novelists John O'Hara, F. Scott Fitzgerald, Mary McCarthy, and William Kennedy; the playwright Eugene O'Neill; and the film actor Spencer Tracy are just a few of the Irish Americans who have enriched the nation with their gifts.

The Germans

For more than two decades after their arrival in North America, the Irish prevailed as the nation's largest immigrant group, but by 1865 that distinction had gone to the Germans. At the end of the century approximately 4.5 million Germans outnumbered the Irish by about 1 million. But Germans had in fact been in the

United States in some numbers since the 18th century. By the time of the revolutionary war in 1776, nearly 225,000 Germans lived in the 13 colonies.

The Germans who arrived during the 19th century hailed from the northern and eastern regions of their homeland: Prussia, Bavaria, and Saxony. Like the Irish, millions of Germans entered the United States through New York City and then dispersed. Yet many stayed in New York where they developed a flourishing Kleindeutschland (Little Germany). Important German communities also grew in the port cities of New Orleans and Baltimore.

Conditions in Germany were not as bad as in Ireland, but there, too, famines, starvation, and poverty were not unknown. Moreover, some Germans looked to America as the home of liberty, both political and religious. In the wake of the abortive revolutions of 1848, when reformers failed to establish a democratic form of government, a number of German radicals fled to America.

They were joined there in the 1870s by a flock of German-speakers who had lived in Russia under the rule of the czars. Under the relatively liberal reign of Catherine the Great, ethnic Germans within Russia—many of whom were Mennonites—had been permitted to follow a set of beliefs that differed from that of the Russian majority. For example, the Mennonite creed opposed on principle all war and military service. In 1855, Czar Alexander II assumed the nation's throne and ushered in an age of repression in Russia, including the forced conscription of the Mennonites. Many among the German-speaking minority responded to this call to arms by migrating to the United States. Upon their arrival in the New World, thousands headed for the Dakotas, where the harsh climate resembled the rough Russian tundra they had known.

Canada also showed an interest in admitting German-speaking people living in Russia. Officials, who considered the Mennonites desirable farmers for their

An advertisement aimed at German immigrants illustrates the many advantages of life in Texas.

Workers raise their steins at the German-owned Peter Brothers Brewery in San Antonio, Texas.

western provinces, encouraged them to settle in Canada. The government gave them special privileges, and as a result several thousand settled in western Canada in the 1870s. More arrived during World War I from Russia and even from the United States when the Mennonites were persecuted because of their opposition to war.

In general, German immigrants sought both economic opportunity and freedom from political oppression at home. Some had hoped to plant German communities, virtual independent states, on American soil, but these schemes came to nothing. In general, emigrants from Germany harbored a more practical ambition: to earn a good living either as tradesmen, artisans, or farmers. For the most part, immigrants succeeded in their aims because they were endowed with a small savings (which they often used to start businesses). They also had the advantage of being skilled laborers and of knowing the rudiments of working the land. Germans entered the American work force as craftsmen, such as bakers, cabinetmakers, and piano builders. Many of these fields also had the added benefit of being unionized, and Germans often rose through union ranks to become leaders. Germans made their mark not only as artisans but as pioneers. Whereas the

Irish had shunned farming, Germans headed for the upper Mississippi and Ohio valleys to establish their own farms. They usually chose their sites carefully, for example, making sure that they settled near forests where they could easily find timber for fuel and for building.

Germans put down roots also in Illinois, Wisconsin, and Missouri. One particularly popular area of settlement for Germans was Texas. In fact, so many Germans lived in west Texas in the 1840s that the state published its laws in German. Wherever they established communities, German immigrants left a legacy of place-names. Thanks to these German forebears, Americans can now pass through Frankfort, Kentucky; Berlin, Wisconsin; and Hamburg, Michigan.

Within Milwaukee, St. Louis, New York, and Cincinnati, Kleindeutschlands appeared, whole communities where the shops catered to German immigrants. German was the language of the streets and commerce,

The Liederkranz *singing society gathers in Wausau, Wisconsin, in 1913.*

and newspapers, clubs, and organizations attempted to keep German culture alive. One observer said of New York's Kleindeutschland, "Life in Kleindeutschland is almost the same as in the Old Country. . . . There is not a single business which is not run by Germans . . . . The resident of Kleindeutschland need not even know English in order to make a living."

The German Americans' efforts to preserve their culture sometimes irked assimilated Americans. Several states with large German populations tried to legally prohibit teachers from conducting classes in a foreign language. In the end, such antiforeign laws were repealed, but the bitter sentiments that had inspired them continued to poison relations between Germans and their neighbors. Anti-German sentiment peaked in the United States during World War I. As American soldiers—many of German descent—arrived on the battlefields of Europe, anti-German hysteria welled up in cities, towns, and rural outposts across America. In Pittsburgh, Pennsylvania, for example, the music of composer Ludwig van Beethoven was banned from public performance. In Boston, the conductor of the Boston Symphony, Dr. Carl Muck, was arrested because authorities irrationally felt he presented a threat to national security.

The outbreak of hostility that accompanied World War I was directed against German Americans of all religions: Lutheran, Catholic, and Jewish. Although the vast majority of 19th-century German immigrants were either Roman Catholic or Lutheran, about 200,000 claimed Jewish heritage. German-Jewish immigrants were usually literate, and many had been small businessmen in Europe. In the United States the largest single settlement was found in New York City, but many German Jews set out across the vast landscape of America to seek their fortune and quickly won a place in the American economy. Many got their start as peddlers and owners of small dry-goods stores and within a generation turned their modest retail ventures into commercial empires. Department stores such as Macy's

and Gimbel's in New York City; F. & R. Lazarus in Columbus, Ohio; Filene's in Boston, Massachusetts; Thalhimer Bros. in Richmond, Virginia; and Meier & Frank in Portland, Oregon, all had Jewish founders.

German Jews excelled not only as tradesmen but as financiers and as the founders of big New York merchant banks. Jacob Schiff, for example, acted as the banker for American financier J. P. Morgan. Financier Otto Kahn established major Jewish banking institutions that became prominent during the late 19th century. A government study in 1889 of 18,000 employed Jews found that one-third were store owners and 15 percent were bankers, with a large number employed as salesmen and commercial travelers. In the 20th century the German-Jewish community of North America was broadened when a wave of refugees from Nazi Germany escaped to the United States and Canada. Many of these immigrants were men and women of outstand-

Adler and Brothers, a Chicago dry-goods store, was founded by a German Jewish immigrant who worked as a peddler until he saved enough money to begin his own business.

ing achievement, such as the Nobel Prize–winning physicist Albert Einstein.

The nation's German-American community encompassed so many diverse groups of people that even those originally from northern European countries other than Germany were often lumped together with German Americans. This was true of Hungarians, Swiss, Austrians, and also of Scandinavian Americans—a sizable ethnic group in their own right.

The Scandinavians

The Danish, Swedish, and Norwegian immigrants who arrived in America from Scandinavia shared many similarities, yet each group was distinct from the others. All had been affected by the transformation of their homeland from an agrarian to an industrial economy. All had suffered from a simultaneous population explosion and land shortage that had sent thousands from the countryside into small villages. These changes—although typical of Europe in general—rocked Scandinavia later than they did other countries. Therefore, the majority of those from this northern corner of Europe began their migration to the New World between 1870 and 1910.

During this era about 150,000 Norwegians—approximately 25 percent of the nation's population—immigrated to the United States. They were accompanied by nearly 1 million Swedes and almost 300,000 Danes. Although the migration of Scandinavians was steady, the portrait of the typical immigrant changed during the years 1870–1910. Families composed the bulk of immigrants at the beginning of this period, but toward the turn of the century, families were overtaken in number by a huge population of single young males looking for a better start in America.

The vast majority of Scandinavians headed west to wheat-growing country in Illinois, Wisconsin, Iowa, Minnesota, the Dakotas, Kansas, and Nebraska. The soil in those areas reminded them of home, and so did

the harsh winters. Most traveled there via a combination of steamboat and horse-drawn wagon. During the
first leg of the journey—which nearly always originated
in New York—immigrants traveled first by boat up the
Hudson River and then up the Erie Canal to Buffalo.
From there they headed west by wagon.

As a group, nearly all Scandinavians dreamed of
owning their own farms, and those not wealthy enough
to buy one immediately after their arrival worked at a
variety of jobs to save money for a down payment. Danish immigrants, for example, tended to get their start
by working as hired hands on dairy farms throughout
Wisconsin, where the majority of Danes settled. In contrast, Norwegians often sought jobs as lumberjacks in
the Far West, as merchant seamen, or as railroad workers. Norwegian Americans helped extend the transcon-
tinental railroad from the Dakotas to the Pacific Coast
during the 1870s. But sometimes jobs for railroad companies involved tasks other than laying tracks. In North
Dakota, for example, railroad companies such as the
Great Northern established "bonanza farms." They
purchased huge plots of land and hired hundreds of
workers to produce tons of wheat that was then sold at
a profit.

Of all the Scandinavian ethnic groups, the Swedish
were the true pioneers who settled the heartland of the
United States. Their log cabins—a uniquely Swedish
contribution to the American landscape—stretched
across Michigan, Indiana, and Ohio. When land be-

*Railroad workers, such as the
ones pictured here in 1883, often
claimed Norwegian origin.*

A Swedish pioneer family poses in front of their sod home in South Dakota in about 1910.

came scarce in the United States toward the end of the 19th century, Swedish pioneers crossed the border into Canada, where they helped tame the vast wilderness of the western provinces. Swedish Americans founded countless rural settlements, but they also lent their enormous energy to urban centers such as Chicago. By the time of World War I, Chicago claimed a larger Swedish population than any city in Sweden except the capital, Stockholm.

Whether in the city or the country, concentrations of Scandinavians gave a distinct Danish, Swedish, or Norwegian flavor to many areas of the upper Midwest. One could hear their languages on the streets and in the Lutheran churches, which were so important to these ethnic communities. First-generation Scandinavians—who tended to be the most devout—sent home for ministers, but in time they founded schools, colleges, and seminaries to train Lutheran ministers in North America. They did not mix or marry outside their own ethnic group at first, but gradually churches and other ethnic institutions became more Americanized, and Norwegian, Danish, and Swedish churches merged, and their members intermarried with other ethnic groups. As a result, millions of Americans now can trace at least one section of their family tree back to Scandinavia.

Germany, Ireland, and the Scandinavian nations furnished the vast bulk of European immigrants before 1880. But immigrants also came from Belgium, the Netherlands, Russia, Wales, and nearly all parts of Europe. Europe, however, was not the only source of new immigrants to the United States. During the late 1800s and throughout the 20th century, several hundred thousand French Canadians made their way south to the United States. In fact, by 1980, the U.S. Census Bureau counted 780,000 Franco-Americans, as the descendants of French Canadians are called in the United States.

As is the case with other immigrant groups, the flow of French Canadians into the United States was linked directly to the U.S. economy. During boom years the demand for workers increased, and states, companies, and the federal government did what they could to encourage the entrance of potential workers into the United States. In leaner times, a once-plentiful supply of jobs vanished without warning, and migration from the north virtually ceased. Sometimes French Canadians were forced to repatriate in order to support themselves.

Members of the French-Canadian Bourgeois family gather in front of their home in Fulford, Quebec, in about 1908.

French Canadians who migrated to the United States before the Civil War did so to work as itinerant laborers during the harvest season or in lumber camps. After the Civil War the demand for industrial workers surpassed the need for agricultural laborers, and French Canadians found jobs in the textile mills of New England, often replacing the Irishwomen who had traditionally served as textile employees. Work in mills typically meant 6-day weeks and 12-hour days. Wages were so low that even the smallest children in the family had to pull their weight and find a job in the mill in order to help make ends meet. At the end of their long shift, families returned to the dark and crowded tenements they called home.

After working for a few years in the United States, a sizable percentage of French Canadians decided to return to their native land. Nevertheless, distinctive French-Canadian neighborhoods arose in New England's industrial areas. Cities like Woonsocket, Rhode Island, and Lewiston and Waterville, Maine, had flourishing French-Canadian populations. Community life in these enclaves revolved around close-knit families and the Roman Catholic church and its offshoots, such as parochial schools.

French Canadians wanted their own priests, and they resented the Irish domination of the church. The

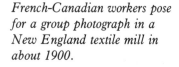

French-Canadian workers pose for a group photograph in a New England textile mill in about 1900.

(continued on page 73)

NEW LIVES IN A NEW WORLD

Immigrants of the 1980s must
face many hurdles before they
can become lawful U.S.
residents. (Overleaf) Illegal
aliens wait in line to register for
a legalization and amnesty
program at the U.S.
Immigration and Naturalization
Service office in Huntington,
California. In New York, a
woman from Guyana receives
information about applying for
U.S. residency from a trained
counselor (right). Some
immigrants find that the greatest
barrier to the Golden Door lies
in gaining entry to the United
States. Above, a Mexican man
evades the U.S. Border Patrol by
wading across the Rio Grande.

After living in the United States for five years, immigrants are eligible to become citizens. Above, immigrants from many lands take the oath of U.S. citizenship in Buena Vista, California.

The daily lives of many Asian
immigrants in New York City
are a blend of old and new
cultures. Two sisters from
India—one in a sari and the
other in a miniskirt—personify
the mix of East and West. On a
fire escape in Chinatown, a
woman dries bokchoy, Chinese
cabbage, on a clothesline
(above). An East Indian family
picnics at the Bronx Zoo (right).

Many immigrants take part in political activity, whether to promote awareness of persecution in their native land or to demonstrate against prejudice in their new country. (Opposite page) Residents of New York City's Chinatown demand an end to labor discrimination and march on behalf of Indochinese refugees. Above, a Filipino American decries the Philippines' Marcos regime.

Immigrant school children learn the rudiments of English from their teacher in a special California public school program.

(continued from page 64)

church hierarchy opposed this idea because they rejected the notion of parishes organized around nationality and tried to Americanize the French parishes, but they never fully succeeded in their aims. In Providence, Rhode Island, in the 1920s, a contest between French-Canadian Catholics and an Irish-American bishop over parish control of finances and the use of French as the language of the liturgy led to a bitter court fight and the bishop's excommunication of several French-Canadian community leaders.

Tension between French Canadians and Irish flared up in other arenas, too. The two groups often competed for the same factory jobs and thus regarded each other with suspicion and hostility. In addition, the Irish and French Canadians held differing philosophies about assimilating into U.S. society. The Irish wanted to Americanize themselves as quickly as possible and resented the French Canadians' drawing attention to the Catholic religion by their insistence on French-speaking priests.

The French Canadians' reluctance to assimilate into the mainstream of American life sometimes provoked the hostility of their neighbors. Yet as people of European background and Caucasians they won acceptance far more easily than immigrants such as the Chinese, who differed dramatically from the white majority both in appearance and in custom.

The Chinese were the first Asians to immigrate to the United States and Canada. In the mid-1800s unskilled Chinese began journeying to the West Coast of the United States in large numbers, arriving just after the discovery of gold in California in 1849. In 1850–1882, more than 300,000 Chinese immigrants—mostly impoverished peasants—crossed the Pacific for North America, lured by the promise of riches. More than 90 percent of those leaving China were male because Chinese social custom mandated that women remain with their families at home.

Some Chinese—unable to raise funds for the voyage—enlisted the aid of a work broker in order to emigrate. As with the indentured servants of the 17th century, the potential immigrants signed contracts guaranteeing that they would work for a certain number of years in exchange for the price of their passage. Arrangements of this sort enabled thousands of Chinese to begin a new life in America. Those immigrants under contract were known as "coolies," a word derived from a Hindu term meaning "unskilled laborer." Chinese bound for the New World first signed on as coolies during the 1840s, when they immigrated to Southeast Asia, South America, and Cuba to act as plantation workers. During the 1850s, the vast majority of coolies chose California as their final destination, but many also traveled to Hawaii. Between 1840 and 1900 about 2.4 million Chinese left their homeland. Many Chinese entered the United States through an immigration station at Angel Island in San Francisco Bay.

From there the majority set out for the gold fields of the West—in California, Nevada, and Oregon where they often met with hostility from white miners and were forced into working the mines that had already been picked over and abandoned. Through enormous

Anti-Asian sentiment in America often led to violence between whites and Chinese. Coal miners in Rock Springs, Wyoming, drove the local Chinese out of town in 1885.

hard work, they managed to extract what gold remained from these lean mines. Their perseverance in the face of adversity seemed only to incite still more hostility on the part of whites, who unleashed a campaign of violence and harassment against the Chinese. In time, the assaults by white miners became so frequent that early Chinese-English phrase books armed the immigrants with such expressions as "They were lying in ambush" and "He was choked to death with a lasso." In Canada, the Chinese lived somewhat more peaceably, but still encountered hostility from whites. Most Chinese Canadians settled near the mines of Vancouver, British Columbia, the region of Canada that was to become their home.

When the gold rush ended in the 1860s, many Chinese immigrants found jobs with the nation's burgeoning railroad industry. They were recruited by the Central Pacific Railroad Company to lay the track that would link America's coasts. Scottish novelist Robert Louis Stevenson wrote of the railroads:

> [a]t each stage of construction, roaring, impromptu cities full of gold and lust and death sprang up and then died away again, and are now but wayside stations in the desert. . . . In these uncouth places pigtailed Chinese pirates worked side by side with border ruffians and broken men from Europe, talking together in a mixed dialect.

Thanks to the work of the Chinese, the Irish, the Norwegians, and other immigrants, the Union and the Central Pacific routes were completed with almost miraculous speed. Twenty thousand laborers lay as many as eight miles of track each day. The feat of American companies was paralleled in Canada, where the Canadian Pacific Railroad hired thousands of Chinese workers. Later, Chinese Canadians claimed that a Chinese immigrant was buried under every mile of the Canadian Pacific.

In 1868 the U.S. government signed the Burlingame Treaty with China in order to ensure the continued immigration of Chinese to the New World. This compact aided powerful railroad companies but in the end fueled a growing movement to exclude Chinese from the United States. American workers resented the Chinese because they were willing to accept less money for performing the same labor as whites. Bitter whites blamed Chinese immigrants for lowering wages and raising unemployment among the mainstream of the American work force. Angry men and women formed anti-Chinese societies and lent their support to politicians who promised to deport Chinese workers. In the 1870s, for example, a nominee of the California Workingmen's party ran for office under the slogan Chinese must go!

During the 1870s, anti-Chinese feeling mounted in America. Opponents of Chinese immigrants made sensational and absurd charges against them, claiming that they were an alien and unassimilable race. In Los Angeles, California; Rock Springs, Wyoming; and Tacoma, Washington, angry mobs marched on Chinese neighborhoods and burned them to the ground, killing many and forcing survivors to flee for their life.

Eventually, the racism exhibited by such mobs spread into the highest levels of the U.S. government. In 1882, Congress passed, and the president signed, the Chinese Exclusion Act, the first and only act to prohibit a specific ethnic group from immigrating to the United States. The Exclusion Act barred Chinese from immigrating to the United States for a period of 10 years. In 1892 the Exclusion Act was extended another 10 years by the Geary Act.

Although the Exclusion Act barred Chinese laborers, it did contain a loophole allowing Chinese from economically privileged backgrounds—mostly merchants and students—to enter the country, as could those who were already here when the ban was enacted and who had returned for a visit to China. Moreover,

A corner of San Francisco's Chinatown in about 1900.

the sons of those few Chinese who were born in the United States and were consequently American citizens, were eligible for admission. Some Chinese-American citizens visited China and announced the birth of a son. Some sons were not really related to the immigrants but claimed to be and were called "paper sons," because their only true link to a Chinese-American father was a forged birth certificate.

American government officials were suspicious of all Chinese desiring entry and especially those declaring themselves to be the sons of American citizens. Immigration inspectors detained thousands at Angel Island for weeks and even months until they could satisfy officials that they were one of the categories of admissible Chinese. In 1888, Congress addressed the problem of paper sons by voting into law the Scott Act, which denied reentry into the United States by any Chinese who left the country to return home even for a visit. The act also declared Chinese immigrants ineligible for citizenship.

Hostility toward the Chinese sometimes grew as intense in Canada's western provinces, the only area of the country with a Chinese populace. In 1884 a Canadian labor union insisted that these immigrants "are a non-assimilating race. Their vices are most disgusting. They turn their sick out to die in the streets, and their lepers to fill our prisons. They control the labour in this city [Victoria]. . . . They are of no benefit to this country." Canada then restricted Chinese immigration, mainly by imposing a tax on Chinese wishing to enter the country and by limiting the number of Chinese permitted on vessels entering Canada.

These laws—triggered by a hatred of the Chinese—marked the beginning of major immigration restriction in North America. But strong anti-immigrant bias was nothing new to the United States. Throughout the 19th century, the white Protestant majority regarded with suspicion their new neighbors—impoverished Irish

An anti-Catholic cartoon from 1871 shows bishops with "crocodile" miters, the liturgical headdress worn by church fathers.

Catholics, French Catholics, Germans, and Chinese, among others—and perceived them as a detriment to the nation. In the 1840s, for example, native-born Protestants organized a secret society called the Order of the Star-Spangled Banner. Members of this order—if questioned by outsiders—replied simply, "I know nothing," and were eventually dubbed the "Know-Nothings." Know-Nothings sought to elect only native-born Americans to office and to require 25 years' residence for U.S. citizenship. Such anti-immigrant sentiments were by no means limited to the United States, as shown by a 19th-century Toronto newspaper, which remarked of the Irish, "Irish beggars are to be met everywhere, and they are as ignorant and vicious as they are poor. They are lazy, improvident, and unthankful; they fill our poorhouses and our prisons, and are as brutish in their superstition as Hindoos."

In the United States, the Civil War served to dampen the flames of nativism. When the war came, immigrants proved themselves to be loyal citizens. In the North, the Irish, even though they did not approve of the abolition of slavery for fear of competition from free black workers, joined the North's armed forces and fought to preserve the Union. Other Northern immigrants did the same. Not until later in the 19th century would nativism become important again, but then it was directed at the new immigrants from southern and eastern Europe and not at the Irish. ∾

A cartoon from The Judge, *a 19th-century publication, reflects the widespread fear that continued immigration would turn the entire nation into an overcrowded tenement house.*

Approximately 27 million immigrants passed through the entry station at Ellis Island during the Great Migration of the late 19th and early 20th centuries.

THE GREAT MIGRATION AND THE NEW IMMIGRANTS

During the 19th century, the Industrial Revolution, which had swept through western Europe, moved to the south and to the east. The economic and social changes that had transformed Great Britain and Germany in the early 1800s now affected Italy, Russia, central and eastern Europe, and the states located in and around the Balkan Mountains—Serbia/Croatia, Romania, Bulgaria, Albania, Greece, and Turkey. Peasants from these regions—squeezed off their land—migrated to the great cities of Europe and to the growing urban centers of North America. For many, the choice lay between migration and starvation. According to one Italian immigrant, quoted in *Ethnic Americans* by David Reimers and Leonard Dinnerstein, "We would have eaten each other had we stayed."

The so-called new immigrants shared many similarities with their predecessors. Like immigrants from western Europe, arrivals from southern and eastern Europe were often recruited to the shores of the United States. During the 1800s individual states, railroad companies, and steamship lines had been primarily re-

Steamship lines often established immigrant dormitories to lodge passengers en route to North America, such as this one at the Atlantic Park Hotel in Southampton, England.

sponsible for the recruiting. In the 1900s, the steamship lines carried almost all the weight of this effort.

These companies did a booming business in the trade of carrying immigrants to North America, and they competed with one another by sending agents all over Europe to find passengers. Employees of the British Cunard Line, for example, met trains as they arrived in port cities and singled out all the passengers who were bound for North America. The company then provided housing for those waiting for their ships and even made kosher—or ritually correct—food available for Jews. The companies' agents could speak a variety of eastern European languages.

During the years of the Great Migration, roughly 1880–1920, western Europeans continued to arrive in North America, but they were eclipsed by peoples from the southern and eastern parts of the Continent. For example, in 1882, the peak year of 19th-century migration, 250,630 Germans arrived in the United States, whereas in 1907, the 20th century's greatest year of influx, only 37,000 Germans, out of a total of 1,285,349 immigrants, arrived on American shores. In all, the Great Migration brought 27 million immigrants to U.S. soil.

The Isle of Tears

As the numbers grew, the federal government took over active control of the immigration process. In 1892 government officials opened the doors to Ellis Island and established an orderly method of deciding which immigrants could stay and which would not be allowed to remain in America. As the qualifications for entrance grew more stringent, so, too, did the screening procedures to which immigrants were subjected. In 1907, for example, Congress passed a law excluding immigrants with physical or mental defects that might affect their ability to earn a living. This legislation also barred those with tuberculosis and children unaccompanied by their parents. Therefore, after 1907 immigrants had to demonstrate their physical health during a thorough medical examination.

All tests were administered by doctors, nurses, and inspectors hired by the government. Immigration officials, along with concessionaires who sold the immigrants steamship tickets and exchanged foreign currency for dollars, were not immune to fraud and scandal. Immigrants threatened with deportation would sometimes have to bribe an Ellis Island employee in order to gain entry to America.

The Ellis Island experience was traumatic for many, and the immigrants called the island "The Isle of Tears." Most knew no English and were confused by the myriad rules and regulations. Inspectors routinely detained about 20 percent of all immigrants for several days to check more thoroughly for disease or to find

Immigrant children cavort in a playground located on top of the processing center at Ellis Island in a photograph dating from about the turn of the century.

A medical examiner at Ellis Island, one of hundreds of government workers employed there, uses a stethoscope to examine an immigrant woman.

sufficient evidence that the newcomers would be able to support themselves financially and not become wards of the state. On occasion, families were temporarily separated while they were trying to satisfy the inspectors that they were eligible to enter. Immigration officials were especially suspicious of women and children who lacked adequate funds. In all, about one percent of those trying to enter were denied permission.

Through years of experience—and the untiring efforts of immigrant advocate groups—Ellis Island became a more efficient and humane place, inspecting and admitting up to 8,000 immigrants a day. More professional officials were appointed, and numerous charitable agencies opened and maintained offices there to protect the immigrants from harassment or unjustified deportation. As a result of improved services, most immigrants spent only a day or so—or even just a few hours—passing through Ellis Island. Once the immigrants were admitted, they sought help and guidance from immigrant aid societies.

These organizations helped the newcomers find housing, buy tickets to destinations outside New York City, and locate friends and family. The aid societies, established along national or religious lines, were first organized in the late 18th century and expanded their activities as the immigrant stream to the United States grew. Among the most prominent was the Hebrew Immigrant Aid Society (HIAS), which in the mid-1980s still lent assistance to Soviet and other late 20th-century Jewish immigrants. Other highly visible societies included two groups founded to help Italian immigrants: St. Raphael's Society and the Society for the Protection of Italian Immigrants.

Arriving in Canada

Canada, too, saw a huge stream of immigrants enter the country, nearly 3 million between 1896 and 1914. But immigrants bound for Canada numbered only a fraction of those entering the United States. In 1913, the peak year of Canadian immigration during the 20th century, the country opened its doors to about 400,000 newcomers, as compared with the 1,197,000 who entered the U.S. immigration station at Ellis Island during the same period of time. As in the United States, a growing number of these new arrivals in Canada hailed from Russia, Italy, and elsewhere in southern and eastern Europe. For example, the number of Italian Canadians rose from 1,000 in 1901 to 67,000 two decades later. By 1921 people of French or British descent composed only 85 percent of the Canadian populace.

In contrast to the United States, Canada had no official immigration station such as Ellis and Angel islands. Instead, Canadian officials inspected boats carrying immigrants when the vessels arrived in ports such as Quebec City, Vancouver, or Montreal. In the 19th century, Canada's immigration policy provided few prohibitions for Europeans, and not until the early 20th century did government officials take a harder look at incoming people. An act passed in 1906 and another in 1910 barred persons considered undesirable, such as those with poor health or those likely to become public charges. And for many years Canadian officials maintained only a casual inspection of Americans entering Canada. Thus, while both the United States and Canada desired new workers and farmers for their expanding economies, Canadians seemed more eager than the Americans for newcomers and lagged behind the United States in enacting immigration restrictions.

Emigrants from Italy

Who were the millions of newcomers from southern and eastern Europe during this era, and why did they emigrate? The largest single nationality was Italian. Before the 1880s, most Italian immigrants came from the more prosperous regions of Italy, located in the north. But toward the end of the 19th century the vast majority

A poster produced by the Canadian government promotes settlement of the country's western provinces.

A newly arrived Italian family stand with their worldly belongings at Ellis Island, sometime near the turn of the century.

came from the south, especially from Sicily, a part of Italy that sits just off the mainland in the Mediterranean Sea. From 1880 to 1910 more than 3 million Italians immigrated to America. Their story most resembles that of the Irish, whom they would encounter in the ethnic urban enclaves springing up within America.

Both the southern Italians and the Irish fled from impoverished agricultural nations that were plagued by high unemployment, overpopulation, inadequate arable land, and famine. Southern Italians—mostly farmers—suffered, too, from falling prices paid for their produce. Most families in southern Italy lived in flimsy houses, with little sanitation and privacy. Landless peasants roamed the highways in search of work that brought them at most the equivalent of 30 cents per day, but often the farmers failed to find even these menial jobs. When word of North America's high wages reached Italians, they came to America in droves. In some villages almost the entire population of young males emigrated to find work in America. Much as the Irish and Chinese had built the nation's canals and railroads, Italians were responsible for the building of New York City's subway system.

The Jewish Americans

Next to Italians the largest group to come to the United States was the Jews. Eastern European Jews shared the poverty of their fellow immigrants, but they differed greatly in their religious heritage and history. Whereas most 19th-century Europeans made their living as farmers—and had done so for generations—Jews were forbidden by law from owning land and so were forced to turn to other enterprises to earn their keep. In addition, they were by and large forbidden to mingle with Christians and were prohibited from settling in whatever country they pleased. In 1880 nearly half the world's Jews—about 4 million—lived in the Russian Empire, restricted to an area known as the Pale of Settlement,

located between eastern Poland and western Russia. These Jews usually lived in isolated villages called *shtetls*.

During the mid- and late 1800s, Jews within the Pale endured a campaign of anti-Semitic terror. Russian soldiers, called cossacks, entered shtetls on horseback and launched pogroms, violent attacks during which entire towns were massacred. During this time even those Jews living beyond the Pale in such countries as Germany were subject to a rash of anti-Semitic legislation and burdened with restrictions on the work they could perform and the places in which they could legally reside. These adverse conditions forced Jews from across Europe to emigrate during the 1880s. In 40 years, from 1880 to 1920, the number of Jews living in the United States rose from about 6,000 to nearly 4 million.

Kishinev, Russia, after a 1903 pogrom in which 50 Jews were killed.

The Work Force of Two Nations

Jews were not the only immigrants to arrive in North America from eastern Europe during the late 19th century. They were accompanied by Poles, Russians, Croatians, Slovaks, and Serbs, among others. Polish and Slavic peoples—originally from present-day Czechoslovakia—did not face starvation, as did the Italians, or pogroms, as did the Jews. Nonetheless, they were oppressed by poverty and tyrannical political regimes.

In the late 19th and early 20th centuries approximately 650,000 Slovaks and 2.5 million Poles made their way to the United States. By the mid-1980s, Americans of Slavic descent numbered between 1 million and 2 million, and those of Polish extraction totaled nearly 8 million. Both these groups flocked to industrial centers in the United States and Canada and worked in booming steel mills and coal mines from Pennsylvania to Ontario.

American industry might not have grown as rapidly as it did without the influx of emigrants from Poland and Slovakia. To a large extent, those Europeans arriving in the late 19th century had little choice about their vocation. The majority arrived well after pioneers had completed the clearing and settling of the American frontier. Thus, immigrants of the early 20th century were forced to pioneer not in America's vast forests and

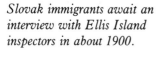

Slovak immigrants await an interview with Ellis Island inspectors in about 1900.

prairies but in the industrial landscape of factories and mines, meat-packing houses, and garment-manufacturing plants (known as sweatshops). In the first decades of the 1900s these new immigrants also joined the ranks of automobile workers who formed the assembly lines at the Ford Motor Company and other car manufacturers.

Canada's pace of industrialization was slower than that of the United States but still drew thousands of immigrants to the nation's provinces. Most ended up in urban centers such as Toronto, Montreal, and Winnipeg, the gateway to Canada's western prairies. Between 1881 and 1911, for example, Winnipeg grew from a town of 8,000 to a city of 136,000. The British proportion of the city's population fell from 84 percent to 59 percent in the same period.

During the early 20th century, the astounding growth of America's cities paralleled that of Canada's. In 1920, for the first time, the census takers reported that more Americans lived in cities than in rural areas. By the 1930s, Chicago had over 3 million residents, and New York City, about 7 million. This swelling in population corresponded directly with the influx of immigrants into America. In fact, in most U.S. cities located outside the South, immigrants and their children made up over half the population—two-thirds in New York. Thus, the inhabitants of the ancient villages and shtetls of Europe now found themselves face-to-face in the dynamic—and often squalid—metropolitan centers of the New World. ❧

The peddlers on Rivington Street—located on New York City's Lower East Side—were a common sight for Jewish and Italian newcomers to Manhattan during the early 20th century.

Residents of a Jewish neighborhood in New York City's borough of Brooklyn congregate in front of the local ice cream shop. The sign with Hebrew lettering is written in Yiddish, the everyday language of most Eastern European Jews.

NEW IMMIGRANTS IN A NEW WORLD

From 1880 to about 1920 millions of new immigrants poured into the cities of America. Although they differed in their ethnicity, religious beliefs, and expectations of life in the New World, they all faced similar challenges during their first days and weeks in North America. The two most crucial tasks were the search for housing and employment. Most immigrants tried to settle among their compatriots in ethnic communities throughout the United States and Canada. Many had kin in these neighborhoods, men and women who had written home, urged fellow villagers to migrate to the New World, and even sent passage money or tickets for steamships.

Thus, like congregated with like: Italians and Jews headed for New York City and Chicago, Slavs made their way to Pittsburgh and—along with Poles—to neighborhoods in Chicago, Buffalo, and, later, Detroit. Greeks moved by the thousands to Chicago and New York. On the West Coast, San Francisco served as the primary locus for Asian newcomers to California. According to some estimates, over 70 percent of the city's population spoke a foreign language by 1916.

This section of Mulberry Street, located in New York City's Little Italy, was popularly called "the Bend." Most city residents considered it the core of Manhattan's immigrant ghetto.

In ethnic districts—labeled Greektown, or Little Italy by Americans of long standing—immigrants saw familiar faces, food, dress, and goods—reminders of the Old World. Yet they also confronted new customs and traditions: those of the mainstream society around them and those of other immigrant groups, who often settled nearby. In America's ethnic enclaves, Greeks, Italians, and Jews, for example, often lived side by side, sharing front stoops and backyard laundry lines.

Squalor in the Cities

Immigrants also shared overcrowded and inadequate housing. New York's famed tenements—where the bulk of the new immigrants to the United States resided—were six- or seven-story buildings with four apartments per floor. These apartments, often shaped like dumbbells, were squeezed side by side, and only the front rooms faced the street, where direct air and light were available. The other rooms looked out over air shafts, which generally allowed in more soot than oxygen. If fresh air was lacking, so were sanitation fa-

cilities. People shared toilets, which frequently overflowed. The problem of filthy neighborhoods was
compounded by erratic garbage collection in the streets.
Open piles of trash—next to which children played—
attracted rats, as did the horse droppings that fouled
the avenues.

Immigrant families, often large in size, could afford
only these small three- or four-room apartments. In order to make ends meet, many families took in lodgers,
who were sometimes, but not always, relatives. The
borders added to the overcrowding, caused in part by
poverty and in part by a huge demand for housing,
which could not be fulfilled overnight. Cramped tenements, coupled with generally unwholesome living conditions, provided the perfect breeding ground for a
varity of epidemics: Mumps, scarlet fever, whooping
cough, and measles regularly took their toll on families,
especially the youngest members.

These health problems were aggravated by the immigrants' low incomes, which prohibited them from
paying for medical care or even having a healthful diet.
Most greenhorns commanded few skills, spoke little
English, and lacked a formal education. Better-paying
jobs eluded them, and so they hired themselves out as
unskilled laborers to mills, factories, and mines in order
to support their families.

*Laundry hangs from clotheslines
behind a row of tenements
located on Roosevelt Street in
New York City.*

Polish-American workers such as these provided the United States and Canada with a pool of unskilled labor for factories and for construction jobs.

In Factory and Mine

Regardless of where they worked, the immigrants found life difficult. Wages were usually low and hours long. The 12-hour day was the norm in the steel industry until the 1920s and, despite this backbreaking labor, workers earned only $2 or $3 dollars per day. This was a low wage, even by the standards of that era. Shoe-shine "boys," often grown men, made less than $200 annually, and sweatshops paid not much more. In 1910, Pittsburgh social workers estimated that families required a weekly income of $15 in order to live above the poverty line, but in reality only one-third of the immigrants living in Steel Town—as Pittsburgh was called—made that much. This situation was paralleled in New York, Chicago, the Canadian city of Toronto, and anywhere else immigrants settled in large numbers.

But immigrants suffered more than low pay in their jobs. During the late 19th and early 20th centuries, working conditions were often dangerous. The industrial masses toiled long hours without proper lighting, ventilation, or safety precautions. Accidents were frequent in steel mills, in mines, and in countless other places. A survey by social workers of Pittsburgh steel-factory employees in the first decade of the 20th century revealed that hundreds of laborers were killed or maimed every year.

As bad as the accidents were, neither the victims nor their families received any financial compensation for the loss of an arm, a leg, or a life. The death or crippling of a breadwinner forced more than 1 family to send young children, including some under 10 years of age, to work. Some immigrant groups, such as the Slovaks and the Poles, accepted this child labor more readily than others because they did not prize education and were willing to withdraw their children from the schools.

In the Pennsylvania mining regions, Slavic boys less than 12 years of age worked above ground sorting coal, and even a few descended into the mines. Among Italians also it was common for boys to work. Some child laborers roamed the streets selling newspapers, and others worked at home sewing garments for large clothing manufacturers. Home sewing work was popularly known as piece work because laborers were paid by the garment rather than by the hour. Social workers often encountered as many as five or six children sewing garments in one room of a tenement. The pay was low, but many families needed this additional income to survive.

The Asian Experience

During the early 20th century, agriculture, not industry, provided the Asian immigrants of the West Coast with their major source of employment. The advent of the refrigerated railroad car in the early 1900s made possible the transportation of a wide variety of produce from the fertile fields of California (and Hawaii) across the country. Hawaii's growers ran farms as big businesses. They hired boatloads of Chinese, Japanese, Korean, and Filipino immigrants to till fields abounding in pineapple and sugarcane, among other fruits and vegetables. Asians usually worked as field hands on these plantations—the West Coast equivalent of coal

Hawaii's sugar industry relied on the labor of Japanese workers, pictured here with a steam-powered plow in the fields of a plantation.

A Filipino boy cuts cauliflower on a large farm in Santa Maria, California, in 1937.

mines or steel factories, from the workers' point of view. In time, some Asian farm workers saved enough of their earnings to buy their own plots of land.

The Japanese transplanted their farming skills from Asia to America with astounding success. Because of legal restrictions, Japanese immigrants owned only about 4 percent of California's farmland, but they produced more than 10 percent of the state's farm crops. They were the first to make rice growing a profitable venture in California. They converted swamps and arid land into productive farms and offered new products such as flowers, celery, and strawberries.

Like the Japanese, Koreans often grew rice, which flourished in the cool climate of northern California. Some Koreans took up vegetable growing and established their own small farms. This work was far preferable to them than the grueling cultivation of pineapples—the main occupation of Korean immigrants newly arrived in America from about 1900 to 1910. Like the Chinese and Japanese before them, the Koreans provided the plantations of Hawaii with their principle source of labor. Koreans found plantation life hard and unrewarding. They were drained by 10-hour workdays and 6-day workweeks. Their exhaustion was not relieved by living conditions, which invariably included squalid housing, isolation, and poor food.

Just as newly arrived Koreans tended to grow a single crop—the pineapple—many Filipinos specialized in the farming of lettuce. But the vast majority of Filipinos were not farmers but migrant workers who followed the harvesting of seasonal crops, picking strawberries in the spring in California and then traveling up north to Washington or Oregon to work in apple orchards in the fall. Once Filipinos had saved enough to settle down, they tended to cluster in such enclaves as Stockton, California, known by whites as Little Manila. In addition, emigrants from the Philippines found employment as domestics, and as line workers in the fish canneries of the Pacific Northwest and Alaska.

Italians as Workers

Immigrants across America tended to be drawn into occupations dominated by their compatriots, just as they were inclined to settle in neighborhoods that were already home to fellow countryfolk. The Italians, for example, dominated the construction trade and provided New York City with 75 percent of its masons, builders, and bricklayers at the turn of the century. Italian women were renowned for their fine needlework and frequently found employment in the city's garment industry, although Italian custom dictated that female family members work only in the home.

Italians usually found jobs with the help of other Italians, frequently friends and relatives from their villages. For Italians, and Greeks as well, labor agents of these nationalities, called *padrones*, were also instrumental in finding work. Padrone was originally an Italian word meaning both "protector" and "owner," and these men usually lived up to both connotations of their name. They guided the non-English-speaking Greeks and Italians into lumber camps, factories, and construction work and found them employment and places to live. Some padrones acted as helpmates to their charges and assisted them in writing letters home or orienting

In 1930 workers in Manhattan—most of them probably Italian immigrants— lay granite blocks on 28th Street between Broadway and Sixth Avenue.

97

themselves in the new country. Other padrones treated the immigrants like slaves: They exercised rigid control over the greenhorns' life, collecting hefty fees for their services. The padrone became less important after 1900 as the immigrant communities grew and states began to regulate labor agents.

The Needle Trades: Jewish Garment Workers

Jews as well as Italians occupied a special niche in the nation's labor force. New York City was the primary home of Jews within the United States, and it was the city's rapidly expanding garment industry that provided most of them with jobs. Jewish laborers accounted for about 70 percent of the city's garment work force on the eve of World War I. These included many young Jewish women, usually single.

In the garment industry, Jews were the leaders in organizing some of the nation's first labor unions, including the Amalgamated Clothing Workers Union and the International Ladies Garment Workers Union. Jewish labor leaders educated workers in the rudiments of strikes and negotiations and initiated a series of successful strikes that led to improved wages and conditions for workers. The union cause gained ground in 1911, when the Triangle Shirtwaist Company—a manufacturer of women's blouses—exploded into flames, killing 154 employees who were unable to excape. The deaths were the direct result of hazardous conditions within the 10-story Triangle building, and the tragedy sparked nationwide outrage at the abuses of company management.

The catastrophes at the Triangle company and others like it ultimately aided the drive for unionization by sparking public sympathy for the plight of unskilled workers. State legislatures began passing laws that detailed factory safety standards and humanized the workplace by specifying a minimum wage and maximum working hours. Labor laws also began to outlaw child

An Eastern European family sews piecework in a Manhattan tenement. The majority of Jewish immigrants in New York found employment in the city's burgeoning garment industry.

labor. Although such legal protections are now taken for granted, they were revolutionary at the time and greatly improved the life of the immigrants who composed much of the unskilled labor force in the country.

Settlement Houses and Schoolrooms

The new immigrants were assisted in a variety of ways by urban reformers. These pioneering social workers organized hundreds of settlement houses, institutions staffed by men and women who offered workshops, libraries, information on health care, and educational programs. Settlement houses were located in poor neighborhoods and helped improve the daily life of the immigrants living there.

Settlement workers and other reformers were in the forefront of a crusade to urge municipal governments to improve the living conditions within immigrant neighborhoods. Among the most active reformers was journalist Jacob Riis. In the 1880s, his accounts of New York's squalid, unhealthy tenements gripped thousands of readers. In 1890 he published his searing account of urban slums *How the Other Half Lives*. Riis lectured nationwide about the evils of tenement housing and the need for legislative reform and community action.

Cities responded to the pleas of urban reformers by building public bathhouses and playgrounds, bringing health care to tenement neighborhoods, improving gar-

Young New Yorkers stand before the Henry Street Settlement, one of the most famous settlement houses of the early 20th century.

bage collection, and passing laws aimed at improving housing in the immigrant neighborhoods. The laws were not always rigorously enforced at first, but in time they improved the life of millions of new immigrants.

For many immigrants salvation from squalor and poverty lay not only in social reform but in education. Some groups, such as Jews, Japanese, Armenians, Czechs, and Greeks, eagerly embraced public education: Adults flocked to night classes, especially those providing English instruction, even after a long day's work. In New York City, the children of immigrants attended the city's free public elementary schools and colleges, such as Hunter College and the City College of New York—one of the nation's most admired institutions of higher education during the early and mid-20th century.

Third- and fourth-generation Americans lauded public education as a means of assimilating the new immigrants into American customs and culture. But some newcomers objected to the Americanization of their offspring. Furthermore, they viewed education as largely irrelevant to the needs of any except the upper classes. This Old World point of view was common among people of European peasant origin, especially

Poles, many other Slavs, and Italians—all of whom had much higher drop out rates than did Jews or Japanese.

New World, Old Values

Many new arrivals in America found themselves at conflict not only with the notion of public education but with mainstream society at large. For some of the older immigrants, in particular, the shock of being uprooted was too traumatic for them to embrace the values of their adopted homeland. These men and women tried not to assimilate into American society but to re-create their homeland within their new surroundings. They retained their native language and refused to adapt their dress and appearance to that of the larger world around them.

This reluctance to learn new ways often brought immigrants into conflict with their American-born and American-reared offspring. The younger generation considered itself American rather than Polish, Italian, or Slavic. They spoke English far more fluently than their parents did and made no secret of their desire to forgo many of the customs of their ancestors. For example, the children of immigrants refused to have matchmakers choose their spouses, as was common in the old country; instead, they wanted to do as Americans did and fall in love with the young man or woman of their choice.

Perhaps, too, first-generation Americans saw assimilation as a means to ready acceptance in a society increasingly hostile toward foreigners. The vast majority of Americans viewed with distrust the many immigrants pouring into eastern and western port cities. By the 1920s, a growing uneasiness about massive immigration to the New World gripped the old stock in both the United States and Canada. This mood of apprehension eventually hardened into hostility and inspired legislation to severely curtail the number of Europeans and Asians entering America and Canada. By the mid-1920s the era of massive immigration had come to an end.

In June 1918, 14 months after the United States entered World War I, an immigrant German woman is fingerprinted at an American police station.

CLOSING THE GATES

World War I was a time of crisis for ethnic Americans. In 1914, when war broke out between European nations, the United States lent no direct support to its allies on the Continent. But by 1917 both America and Canada had joined in the war effort. Ethnic minorities of all backgrounds came under new scrutiny in North America because mainstream Americans and Canadians believed that newcomers would side with their native land in time of war. Thus, immigrants were forced to prove their loyalty toward their adopted country.

During this era, German Americans bore the brunt of antiforeign feeling in America. Nearly every person of German descent was subject to a barrage of hostility and abuse, none more so than Robert Prager. On the night of April 4, 1918, a year after the United States declared war against Germany, a group of coal miners from Illinois accused a co-worker named Robert Paul Prager of being a German spy. They dragged him from his home and forced him to kiss the American flag and to sing patriotic songs in front of a violent mob. They then hung him from a tree.

Prager's death was the culmination of a year of harassment of German Americans. Citizens of German descent were publicly flogged or tarred and feathered. Their homes and schools were frequently vandalized.

Many German Americans changed their names to English-sounding ones, from Schmidt to Smith, for example, in order to avoid persecution. Although German Americans were by far the most harassed of all European immigrant groups, they were not the only ones resented and mistrusted by Americans of long standing. And the ill treatment of German-American citizens had repercussions throughout the immigrant community as newcomers of other nationalities realized the intensity of antiforeign feeling in North America.

Legislated Prejudice

After World War I, ill-founded rumors that millions of Europeans were ready to descend upon American shores spread across the country. This hearsay alarmed American workers—who feared foreign competition for jobs—and thereby aggravated nativist hostility. Antagonism toward foreigners was reflected in such reactionary publications as the *Dearborn Independent*, a newspaper owned by auto magnate Henry Ford. Ford, a known anti-Semite, encouraged the paper to print stories about a Jewish plot to rule the world.

Amid this atmosphere of bigotry, the U.S. Congress moved to reduce drastically the number of immigrants arriving from southern and eastern Europe each year. Legislators looked for legal means of barring "undesirable" nationalities from U.S. shores. In 1921, Congress set a limit of approximately 358,000 on the number of Europan immigrants it would allow to enter the country each year. For the first time, the United States instituted a quota system based on a mathematical formula: Each nation was allowed to send over a group of immigrants equal in number to three percent of persons of that nationality already living in the United States. For example, for every 100 Polish Americans already living on U.S. soil, 3 Poles would be allowed to enter the country. This quota system resulted in a drastic reduction in the number of immigrants arriving annually.

Stripped!   By J. H. Cassel

This cartoon from the June 12, 1917, edition of the Morning World Daily Magazine *dramatizes the unfounded distrust many Americans felt toward immigrants during World War I.*

In 1924, Congress enacted the Johnson-Reed Immigration Act, which further limited the number of foreigners allowed to enter the United States. Now only 2 Poles, for example, would be allowed to enter the nation for every 100 Polish Americans already living here.

In 1927 the Johnson-Reed Immigration Act was superseded by a national-origins provision. The Eastern Hemisphere was alloted a total of about 150,000 immigration visas. Each nation received a number of spots, based on that proportion of America's white population that was composed by people of that national origin.

The numbers alloted to each nation speak loudly for American attitudes of the 1920s. Great Britain alone received nearly half of the 150,000 places for immi-

The Ku Klux Klan, a racist secret society, parades in Springfield, Ohio, in 1923. The Klan was originally an anti-black society founded by southerners following the Civil War, but in the 20th century the organization also began persecuting foreign-born Americans, especially Jews and Catholics.

grants, and Great Britain, Ireland, and Germany together were allowed to send two-thirds of all America's new immigrants. Italy, the nation that had sent the largest number of immigrants in recent years, was permitted less than 6,000 annually. By way of comparison, in the early 20th century, Italian immigrants numbered over a quarter of a million annually. In 1924, Congress further reduced immigration by passing the Oriental Exclusion Act, which banned immigration from Asia.

Congress had not included the Western Hemisphere under the national-origins system. Hence, Mexicans and Canadians were not limited to a numerical quota, although like all immigrants they had to pay a head tax and were subject to a long list of restrictions. For example, Mexicans and Canadians carrying contagious diseases such as tuberculosis found themselves barred from entry. When the new quota system was put into effect and emigration from Europe slumped, American industry found itself with a shortage of available cheap labor and turned to Mexico and Canada to fill the void. As emigration from Europe decreased, that from south of the U.S. border increased rapidly.

The Mexican Americans

The nation's first Mexican Americans were actually refugees from the Mexican-American War, a two-year armed conflict between the United States and its southern neighbor. In 1848, Mexico lost nearly one-half of its territory under the terms of the Treaty of Guadalupe Hidalgo, which ended the war. The United States won the present-day states of California, Nevada, Texas, Utah, New Mexico, Colorado, Wyoming, and parts of Arizona. The U.S. government agreed to take responsibility for the thousands of Mexicans living in what was now U.S. territory. It gave these people the choice of becoming U.S. citizens or moving south, back into Mexico proper. Nearly 80 percent of the Mexicans chose to stay, and they became the first true Mexican Americans.

In the late 19th and early 20th centuries, Mexican Americans found jobs building and repairing railroad lines and in mining. They were soon joined by thousands of new Mexican immigrants to the United States. During this period Mexico vacillated between phases of revolution and political stability. Such imbalances in the nation's domestic affairs adversely affected the region's economy and sent thousands of jobless Mexican citizens northward in search of employment. In

A Mexican emigrant passes through Nuevo Laredo, Mexico, in 1912 en route to the United States.

A Mexican cotton picker in California's San Joaquin Valley in 1936 relaxes for a moment.

1890–1900 the Mexican population in the United States increased from 75,000 to an estimated 562,000.

During World War I—as immigration to the United States from Europe dropped sharply—the United States relied on Mexico to supply a steady stream of workers into the country. In the 1920s the U.S. economy boomed, and the country easily absorbed the nearly half million Mexican immigrants who entered the United States officially and the half million who came illegally in order to avoid the head tax levied against all immigrants. These men and women constituted the first major group of illegal or undocumented aliens to enter America.

Like those Mexicans who came before, they sought employment in the growing agricultural regions of the Southwest, especially California and Texas. However, some Mexicans headed for urban centers like Kansas City, Missouri, Detroit, and Chicago. There they found unskilled jobs in industry. Employers were eager to hire these workers, whom they paid scandalously low wages. But Mexican immigrants—who were usually poor and uneducated—accepted American wages of a dollar a day, which were still much higher than wages in Mexico. Many migrants worked for only a few months in the United States and returned home with their savings.

In 1929 the riches of the 1920s disappeared virtually overnight when the stock market crashed. America's economy was shattered, and millions suddenly found themselves out of work. Many Mexicans were forced to give up their jobs to white Americans, and in the last months of 1929 nearly 85,000 Mexican workers voluntarily left the United States. Another 75,000—living in California—reluctantly returned home when threatened with deportation. The Mexican government cooperated with American authorities in their deportation of Mexicans. Within a decade several hundred thousand people were repatriated to their Mexican homeland.

The outbreak of World War II reversed the ailing U.S. economy. Defense plants boomed, and American industry again turned to Mexico to fill its labor pool.

In 1942 the American and Mexican governments negotiated an agreement whereby Mexico would supply contract workers, known as *braceros* (hired hands), to the United States. After the war ended, the two governments extended the bracero program so that American growers in California would have a ready supply of farm workers at their disposal. Between its inception in 1942 and its end in 1964, the bracero program brought a total of 5 million Mexicans into the United States.

Hitler's Refugees

The advent of World War II brought hundreds of thousands of Mexicans into the United States. Even as the United States opened its doors to its southern neighbors, it firmly shut them to Europeans wanting to immigrate. The triumph of Nazi party leader Adolf Hitler in 1933 and the subsequent persecution of Jews and others in Nazi Germany prompted many Germans Jews to flee in panic from their homeland. In addition, when the Nazis took over Austria and Czechoslovakia, thousands of citizens of these countries had to leave in order to save their life.

As growing numbers of Europeans wished to immigrate to the United States and Canada, both nations were faced with the issue of how many refugees to admit. Although the economic depression that had shaken both countries had lifted somewhat by the late 1930s, unemployment was still high, and jobs were difficult to find. Thus, many Americans and Canadians advocated a tight enforcement of the immigration laws. Worry about unemployment was coupled with considerable prejudice against refugees, especially Jews. In both the United States and Canada anti-Semitic groups rallied against allowing Jewish victims of Nazi Germany into America.

As a result, neither the United States nor Canada made much effort to modify their immigration policies to assist refugees. About 500,000 people entered the

In 1939 nearly 1,000 Jews escaped Nazi Germany aboard the ocean liner St. Louis, *pictured here, but they were refused entry into several countries in both North and South America, including the United States and Canada.*

United States during the 1930s, and approximately 200,000 of these were Jewish refugees. Canada did even less to give asylum to those fleeing persecution. Several groups urged the government to relax restrictions and began to raise funds to ensure that newcomers would not become welfare cases, but they could not influence the government to relax restrictions against refugees. In the end, the Canadian government granted asylum to only about 5,000 European Jews.

An American Identity

As virtually unrestricted emigration from Europe came to an end, what happened to the immigrants and their children? The sharp decline in immigration aided the process of assimilation. No longer were large numbers of non-English-speaking Europeans arriving and bringing with them the customs of the Old World. Thus, ethnic neighborhoods lost the steady reinforcement of Old World culture that had characterized the period of massive immigration. As an increasing number of immigrants learned English, they began to adopt a new identity as Americans.

World War II also proved a strong force for Americanization. More than 16 million Americans—women and men of all ethnic backgrounds—served in the armed forces during the war. For many, the war was a catalyst for their assimilation into American society. Children of immigrants were thrust into close contact with members of many other ethnic groups, including fourth- and fifth-generation Americans. Besides, ethnic Americans were eager to prove their loyalty to the United States, and many gladly left the vibrant ethnicity of urban ghettos behind them.

But not all Americans received a ready welcome into the country's armed forces. Japanese Americans found themselves barred from defending their country against their ancestral land. Their selective service classification was IV-C, meaning not acceptable for military service

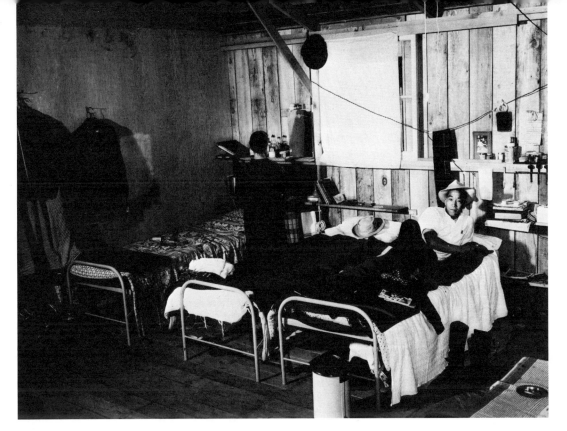

because of ancestry. After some prodding from Japanese civil rights organizations, an all-Japanese army group—the 442nd Regimental Combat Team—was formed in January 1943. These soldiers proved to be the most decorated unit in the history of the American military. The approximately 30,000 soldiers in this division collectively won 3,600 Purple Hearts, 810 Bronze Stars, 342 Silver Stars, 47 Distinguished Service Crosses, and 6 distinguished unit citations.

Civilian members of the Japanese-American community fared much worse during World War II. After the attack by Japan on Pearl Harbor in December 1941, pressure mounted in California to remove and intern the state's Japanese Americans. Finally, in February 1942, President Franklin Roosevelt issued an order to intern all Japanese Americans living on the West Coast. Although military security provided a rationale for this racially biased order, not a single Japanese American was ever found guilty of espionage. In all, more than

A Japanese American reclines in a relocation center in Salinas, California, in 1942.

110,000 Japanese Americans, including about 70,000 who were born in the United States, were penned into relocation centers—essentially, concentration camps, complete with barbed wire and armed guards.

The Postwar Era

In 1945, at the close of World War II, the nation embarked on a new period of economic expansion that spanned three decades. Immigrants, their children, and their grandchildren shared in the prosperity. Many veterans attended college on the GI Bill of Rights (a program of financial assistance for World War II veterans) and entered the professional and managerial ranks of the nation. They also moved to the newly built suburbs, leaving behind the immigrant ghettos for the next wave of newcomers.

The movement to the suburbs further weakened ties to ethnicity as residents from vastly different family

These Lithuanian refugees were photographed as they traveled by boxcar through Genoa, Italy, in 1948. They would ultimately be relocated to Canada. Hundreds of thousands of Europeans displaced by World War II found refuge in North America.

Businesses catering to immigrants seeking naturalization dominate this street corner near the New York City offices of the U.S. Department of Immigration and Naturalization.

backgrounds mingled in a casual way their parents would have found impossible. During the late 1950s and early 1960s, the boundaries separating Protestants from Catholics, Jews from Italians, and blacks from whites began to disappear. On a national level, the country voted a Catholic chief of state into office and declared war on the racist policies of segregation that had for 100 years relegated black Americans to the role of second-class citizens. On a personal level, Americans broadly increased their own social circles. Intermarriage between national and religious groups became the norm. On campuses—and in jobs—Americans of European, Asian, Hispanic, and African ancestry came together to study or work in institutions that had once excluded them. The process of assimilation was a gradual one for the descendants of immigrants and is by no means complete, but clearly the third and now fourth generations lived in a different world than their ancestors who first set foot on American soil. ✎

The Gasthalter family, refugees from Poland, arrive in New York in 1953. Chaim Gasthalter (with beard) spent most of World War II in prison camps.

A NEW WAVE OF IMMIGRANTS

The most recent installment in the story of immigration to North America bears little resemblance to the chapters that have come before. Men and women who had once undertaken week-long journeys to the New World via steamship now step on an airplane and arrive in the United States or Canada within hours of their departure. Immigrants had once learned about the "land of milk and honey" from letters sent home. But now they have only to switch on their television sets to see shows such as "Dallas" and "Dynasty," which portray a Hollywood image of American wealth and opulence. Thus, millions of men and women living in impoverished countries dream of sharing in the abundant prosperity of the United States.

In the late 1900s, for the first time in U.S. history, the vast majority of immigrants arrived in the United States not from Europe but from economically underdeveloped, or Third World, countries in Asia, Latin America, the Caribbean, and Mexico. The 21 nations now sending the greatest number of immigrants to the United States are Canada, Mexico, Costa Rica, El Salvador, Guatemala, Honduras, Nicaragua, Colombia, Ecuador, Peru, the Dominican Republic, Haiti, Jamaica, Nigeria, India, Iran, Korea, the Philippines, Thailand, Greece, and Italy.

Newcomers to the United States now differ not only in their nation of origin but in their status. The peasant populations that once composed the main body of immigrants have been replaced by a more diverse social group. Now a significant number of those entering the nation are professionals from middle-class families, seeking greater career opportunities in America. The demand for American immigration visas from all segments of society has become so strong that the U.S. government can not possibly accommodate all the applicants. Therefore, many foreigners enter the United States however they can—by sneaking across the borders or by obtaining student or visitor visas—and then remain illegally on U.S. soil. The 20th century has seen an increase, too, in the scores of refugees from war-torn nations who seek asylum in the United States.

The myriad changes in immigration policy and population since World War II can all be traced back to the 1940s. After World War II both Canada and the United States reversed the restrictive policies of the previous decades and adopted a more generous attitude toward potential immigrants. The first people to benefit from liberalized immigration policies were postwar European refugees. Between 1948 and 1952 the United States admitted nearly 400,000 victims of war under the Displaced Persons Law, passed in 1948. In 1953, Congress amended this legislation to allow in an additional 200,000 people. During the same period, Canada admitted about 165,000 refugees, most of whom came from Eastern Europe.

In truth, the loosening of the many immigration restrictions of the 1920s began while World War II was still in progress. During the war, the United States repealed the Chinese Exclusion Act and admitted a small number of Chinese immigrants. This was accomplished largely because of foreign policy concerns. The United States was allied with China during its struggle against Japan, and many Americans in government believed that banning Chinese immigration insulted the coun-

In 1956 U.S. president Dwight Eisenhower sent his personal plane to Munich to greet 21 exiles from Hungary and bring them to the United States to begin a new life.

try's new ally. The reversal of the Chinese Exclusion Act marked a new phase of American immigration laws. For the first time, domestic policy regulating newcomers became an extension of the nation's foreign policy.

Still, not all Americans favored a liberalized immigration policy. Adversaries of this new trend cited many reasons—mostly economic—for their opposition to a new influx of foreigners, but their arguments were effectively rebutted by scholars and religious and political leaders, who argued that the United States carried new responsibilities in its position of world leader. They asserted that millions across the globe would be looking to America as a symbol of social and political freedom.

President Harry Truman was one leader who well understood that America's immigration regulations would have repercussions around the world. In 1952, Congress passed the McCarran-Walter Immigration Act, which created a new quota system that allotted every country in the world a minimum quota of 100 persons but gave the nations of northern and western Europe many more spaces than the minimum. Truman, who opposed the bill as too restrictive to southern and eastern European countries, opposed it and told Congress:

> Today we have entered into an alliance, the North Atlantic Treaty Organization, with Italy, Greece, and Turkey, against one of the most terrible threats mankind has ever faced [communism]. We are asking them to

join us in protecting the peace of the world. We are helping them to build their defenses and train their men in the common cause. But through this bill we say to their people: You are less worthy to come to this country than Englishmen or Irishmen.

Throughout the 1950s and early 1960s, Congress continually had to create new legislation to grant entry to greater numbers of immigrants than were allowed to enter under the McCarran-Walter Immigration Act. In 1956, for example, Soviet tanks rolled into Budapest to quell a nationwide uprising within Hungary. In the aftermath of political defeat, about 200,000 Hungarian revolutionaries fled their homeland, and U.S. president Dwight D. Eisenhower used his presidential authority under the immigration laws to grant amnesty to about 38,000 Hungarians. Canada took in approximately the same amount.

Widespread sympathy for the Hungarian refugees sparked a new debate as to whether or not America should be a haven for political refugees. President John F. Kennedy felt strongly that the United States should welcome this role. In 1963 he led a campaign to liberalize the quota system established under the McCarran-Walter Immigration Act. After Kennedy's assassination later that year, his successor, Lyndon Johnson, carried forth the effort to enact a new immigration bill.

President Lyndon Johnson signs the 1965 Immigration Bill into law beneath the Statue of Liberty.

For two years Johnson championed new legislation, and his tireless work resulted in the Immigration Act of 1965, which he signed into law at the foot of the Statue of Liberty in October of that year. The Immigration Act abolished the old national-origins quotas and instead allowed people to enter the United States on a first-come, first-served basis. The bill established an annual limit of 120,000 immigrants for the Western Hemisphere. The bill also permitted 170,000 immigrants from outside the Western Hemisphere and limited immigration from any one country to 20,000. (In 1978 the hemispheric quotas were to be revised into a single global quota of 290,000.) The 1965 Immigration Act gave priority to those immigrants with close relatives in the United States, political refugees, and those with occupational skills—such as the ability to practice medicine—needed in the country.

Beyond Braceros

The new immigration act greatly increased the number of people from Latin American, Asian, and Caribbean countries living in the United States. But no ethnic groups altered American society as dramatically as those of Hispanic origin. The fastest-growing segment of the U.S. population, Hispanics in 1987 numbered about 17 million and were the second-largest American minority, behind black Americans. This figure probably underestimates the nation's Latin American population because the federal government can not fully account for the millions of illegal aliens from Mexico, the Caribbean, and Central America now living in the United States. By the mid-1980s nearly every state in the union could point to visible growth of its Hispanic population.

Of all Latin American nations, Mexico has sent by far the largest number of people north across the U.S. border. Since 1950 about 2 million Mexican immigrants have legally entered the United States, most settling in California, Arizona, New Mexico, and Texas. As of

Would-be Mexican immigrants attempt an illegal entry into the United States by crossing the Rio Grande. The popularity of this method of entry gave rise to the derogatory term wetback *for illegal Mexican immigrants.*

A volunteer teacher at Fort Chaffee, Arkansas, in 1980 instructs a class of Cuban immigrants in English as they await processing by U.S. government officials.

1987 the U.S. Census Bureau estimated the number of Americans of Mexican descent at over 10 million.

Undocumented migration from Mexico has also proved enormous. Mexicans wanting to enter the United States have done so by swimming across the Rio Grande or by hiding in the trunks of cars or on trains. Sometimes attempts at crossing the border have proved fatal, as with the 18 illegal immigrants who suffocated to death in a railroad boxcar during the summer of 1987. Mexicans have devised many ways of avoiding the regulations and personnel of the U.S. Immigration and Naturalization Service, the government agency responsible for overseeing immigration to America. Pregnant Mexican women, for example, sometimes cross the border into Texas and give birth on the American side, knowing that their child will then be a U.S. citizen. At the time that infant turns 21, he or she will be able to sponsor Mexican family members wanting to migrate to the United States.

Just as Mexicans compose the vast majority of Hispanics in the Southwest, Cubans dominate the Hispanic community of the Southeast. A majority of the nearly 1 million Cuban Americans now living in the United States first entered the country as political refugees during the early 1960s. Cubans began flooding into America in 1959 when a Communist revolution led by Fidel Castro forced thousands to flee their homeland. Most sought exile only 150 miles away in Miami, Florida, where they found menial jobs in tourist hotels, restaurants, and in the homes of wealthy Floridians. Some of these refugees moved up into the ranks of Miami's wealthiest and most influential citizens. From their neighborhood, Little Havana, they formed a new and important segment of the state's population, transforming Miami from an economically depressed resort town to a thriving center of trade and finance.

If Cubans are distinguished by their relative affluence among Hispanic groups, Puerto Ricans are known for their perseverance in the face of grueling poverty. Unlike Mexicans or Cubans, Puerto Ricans are not immigrants but American citizens who began their major migration to the United States—mainly to New York City—after World War II. The history of Puerto Ricans in New York parallels that of the Jewish and Italian immigrants of another era. Puerto Ricans, sometimes referred to as "Newyoricans," entered the labor force as unskilled factory workers. They lived in such poor ethnic enclaves as the Lower East Side, which had been abandoned by the offspring of early-20th-century immigrants. As of 1987 about 2 million Puerto Ricans lived on the U.S. mainland.

Immigrant Legislation in the 1980s

The remarkable increase in the Hispanic population of the United States was paralleled by a rise in the number of individuals in many ethnic groups in America: Caribbean Americans from Trinidad, Jamaica, and Haiti; Asians from Hong Kong, the Philippines, and Korea; Indo-Chinese arriving in the aftermath of the Vietnam War in the mid-1970s.

Many of these newcomers were refugees rather than immigrants. According to a definition put forth by the United Nations, refugees include all individuals rendered homeless by racial, religious, political, or social persecution. Of all refugee groups entering America,

Vietnamese refugees aboard the overcrowded and unseaworthy fishing boat they used to escape their nation's communist government. The plight of the boat people attracted the attention of the world's press and helped increase public awareness of Southeast Asian refugees.

the largest during this period was the Indo-Chinese—Cambodians, Vietnamese, and Laotians—about 900,000 of whom poured into the country between 1975 and 1988.

The arrival of so many refugees prompted Congress and President Jimmy Carter to pass a new refugee act in 1980. Under this law, 50,000 refugees were to be admitted annually, and additional numbers were to be granted a special amnesty by the president if he deemed it in the national interest. The Refugee Act of 1980 did not solve what many believed was a refugee crisis within America. Far more than 50,000 people annually wanted to enter the nation, and many did so by illegal means.

Immigration officers and many political leaders argued that a new law was needed to check the flow of illegal immigration. These leaders insisted that undocumented workers took jobs from Americans and drove wages down. Some officials added that they believed that illegal aliens used social services such as schools and medical care that cost the American taxpayers considerable amounts of money. After much debate, in 1986 Congress passed the Immigration Reform and Control Act, which outlawed the employment of illegal aliens and gave amnesty to those who had come before 1982 and had been living here ever since. Those who came after, if caught, would be deported.

Unlike the United States, Canada did not have a large border with a poor neighbor to supervise, but it nonetheless did have to face the refugee issue. By the 1980s, Toronto was home to most of the world's ethnic groups, and the city contained a multitude of ethnic newspapers, organizations, restaurants, churches, and clubs. A book published in 1984 celebrating the city's sesquicentennial anniversary reported on more than 40 ethnic groups in Toronto. One historian wrote that the most salient feature of Toronto in 1985 was "its role as a preferred target of migration for people from every corner of the globe, its polyethnic character and its reputation for tolerance of human variety."

For several decades prior to the 1980s, the Canadian immigration service maintained a generous policy of allowing those who managed to enter Canada to claim asylum. Once the United States passed the 1986 immigration act, many illegal immigrants tried to cross into Canada, which led the Canadian government to tighten its policy in an attempt to maintain control of its borders.

Today, Canada and the United States share a similar concern about immigration. Each year, millions of people throughout the world are uprooted by war, revolution, political oppression, and natural disaster, and millions more live in dire poverty. Of course, not all these people want to come to the United States or Canada, but many do. Both truly nations of immigrants, the United States and Canada will have to decide to what extent that will continue to be so in the decades to come. ✑

Jesus Antonia Arias, a Peruvian living in New York City, is granted a temporary resident identification card by the Immigration and Naturalization Service office. The card was issued under the 1987 immigration law, which granted amnesty to illegal aliens who were willing to reveal their identity to authorities.

FURTHER READING

Chen, Jack. *The Chinese of America: From the Beginnings to the Present*. New York: Harper and Row, 1981.

Dinnerstein, Leonard, and David M. Reimers. *Ethnic Americans: A History of Immigration*. New York: Harper and Row, 1987.

Ewen, Elizabeth. *Immigrant Women in the Land of Dollars: Life and Culture on the Lower East Side, 1890–1925*. New York: Monthly Review Press, 1985.

Glazer, Nathan, and Daniel Moynihan. *Beyond the Melting Pot: The Negroes, Puerto Ricans, Jews, Italians, and Irish of New York City*. Cambridge: Harvard University Press, 1970.

Kessner, Thomas, and Betty Boyd Caroli. *Today's Immigrants, Their Stories*. New York: Oxford University Press, 1982.

Meier, Matt S., and Feliciano Rivera. *The Chicanos*. New York: Hill and Wang, 1972.

Miller, Kerby. *Emigrants and Exiles: Ireland and the Irish Exodus to North America*. New York: Oxford University Press, 1986.

Morawska, Ewa. *For Bread with Butter*. Cambridge, England: Cambridge University Press, 1985.

Reimers, David M. *Still the Golden Door: The Third World Comes to America*. New York: Columbia University Press, 1985.

INDEX

PICTURE CREDITS

We would like to thank the following sources for providing photographs: American Jewish Historical Society: pp. 26, 79; AP/Wide World Photos: p. 117; Barker Texas History Center, University of Texas at Austin: p. 55; Bostonian Society, Old State House: p. 38; Boston Public Library, Print Department: p. 54; George Henry Boughton, *Pilgrims Going to Church,* detail, New-York Historical Society: pp. 12–13; Antoinette Bourgeois Private Archives, Dimond Library, University of New Hampshire: p. 63; Chicago Historical Society: p. 39; Chicago Jewish Archives: p. 59; Michael Grecco/Picture Group: p. 65; *Harper's Weekly:* p. 74; Haynes Foundation Collection, Montana Historical Society: p. 61; *Illustrated London News:* p. 47; Imperial Tobacco Company: p. 21; President Lyndon Baines Johnson Library: p. 118; Corky Lee: pp. 68, 70, 71; Mrs. Sam Liberto, copy from the Institute of Texas Cultures at San Antonio: p. 56; Library of Congress: pp. 14, 18, 29, 34–35, 41, 50, 51, 53, 77, 78, 86, 89, 105, 106, 107, 108, 111; Stephanie Maze/Woodfin Camp: p. 72; Minnesota Historical Society: p. 62; Museum of American Textile History: p. 64; Museum of the City of New York: p. 83; National Archives: pp. 80–81, 82, 84, 113; National Archives of Canada: p. 31; New-York Historical Society: pp. 33, 37; New York Public Library Picture Collection: pp. 23, 30, 88; New York State Historical Association, Cooperstown: p. 15; *New York Times:* p. 123; PAR/NYC: p. 69; Provincial Archives of British Columbia: p. 44; Public Archives of Canada: p. 85; Rare Book Division, New York Public Library, Astor, Lenox and Tilden Foundations: pp. 19, 20, 22; Ricki Rosen/Picture Group: p. 66; Greg Smith/Picture Group: p. 66; Special Collections Division, University of Washington Libraries: p. 43; State Historical Society of Wisconsin: p. 57; UPI/Bettmann Newsphotos: pp. 102–3, 109, 112, 114–15, 119, 120, 121; Joy Wolf/Picture Group: p. 67; YIVO Institute for Jewish Research: p. 87.

DAVID M. REIMERS is a professor of history at New York University. He has written a number of books on ethnic history, including *White Protestantism and the Negro* and, most recently, *Still the Golden Door: The Third World Comes to America.* He is currently at work on an ethnic history of New York City.

DANIEL PATRICK MOYNIHAN is the senior United States senator from New York. He is also the only person in American history to serve in the cabinets or subcabinets of four successive presidents—Kennedy, Johnson, Nixon, and Ford. Formerly a professor of government at Harvard University, he has written and edited many books, including *Beyond the Melting Pot, Ethnicity: Theory and Experience* (both with Nathan Glazer), *Loyalties,* and *Family and Nation.*